The Duchess of Malfi

&

A Streetcar Named Desire

A Study Guide for
WJEC Eduqas A level English Literature

Izzy Ingram

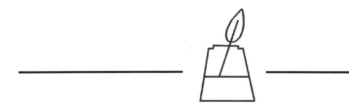

Notable
www.notableguides.co.uk

Notable

www.notableguides.co.uk

Notable is a brand new company, producing textbooks and study guides for the new A-Level courses. Whilst other textbooks give you a general overview of a topic or subject, our guides are tailored to meet the requirements of your exam board, so that you know exactly what do in order to achieve the very best grade possible.

For revision tips and tricks, and to have your say on what we write next, follow us on social media:

Follow us on Facebook

@notableguides

Follow us on Instagram

@notable_guides

Contents

What to expect from this guide

This guide has been written for A-Level students studying English Literature with WJEC Eduqas. For this qualification, you have three different papers to sit: Poetry (Component 1), Drama (Component 2) and the Unseen (Component 3). Component 4 is a coursework essay (non-exam assessment).

This guide has been written for section B on the Component 2: Drama paper. In this section, candidates must <u>compare a play that was written before 1900 with a play that was written after 1900</u>. There are a number of combinations to choose from, but this guide has been written to assist students studying the following pairing:

<u>Pre-1900 text</u>: *The Duchess of Malfi*, by John Webster (c.1613). The exam board recommends the Methuen Drama edition.

<u>Post-1900 text</u>: *A Streetcar Named Desire*, by Tennessee Williams (1947). The exam board recommends the Penguin Classics edition.

Some key points to bear in mind for this paper:

- This is a **closed-book** examination. You will <u>not</u> have copies of the play with you whilst you sit the paper. Therefore, it is vital that you learn some key quotations.

- You will answer **one question** from a choice of two.

- Altogether, the exam lasts for two hours, and you have **one hour** for this half of the paper. It is very important that you leave enough time to write this essay fully. Equally, if you decide to do this half of the paper first, you must ensure that you leave one hour for Section A, since this is also worth 60 marks.

- You have **five assessment objectives** to address in your essay. The tables on pages 6 and 7 provides further information on these. *The text in italics comes directly from the WJEC Eduqas specification.*

AO1	10 marks	*Articulate, informed, personal and creative responses to literary texts, using associated concepts and terminology, and coherent, accurate written expression.* In essence, this assessment objective requires students to <u>write well</u>. Candidates must: - keep spelling and grammatical errors to a minimum - use relevant literary terms - use an academic register - organise your essay in a sensible and coherent way - be fully engaged with the question throughout
AO2	10 marks	*Analyse ways in which meanings are shaped in literary texts.* AO2 is traditional literary analysis. Candidates must: - refer to relevant quotations from the plays - analyse the playwright's use of language - analyse the playwright's use of dramatic techniques - demonstrate an understanding of underlying meanings

AO3	10 marks	*Demonstrate understanding of the significance and influence of the contexts in which literary texts are written and received.*
		This is exactly what the exam board say it is: you must discuss the context in which the plays were written or received, and, for the highest marks, this should be relevant and serve to further your analysis.
AO4	**20 marks**	**Explore connections across literary texts.**
		You must consider similarities and differences between *The Duchess of Malfi* with *A Streetcar Named Desire*. Look at the number of marks available: it is <u>double</u> that of any other assessment objective.
AO5	10 marks	*Explore literary texts informed by different interpretations.*
		There is never one way in which a text can be understood, and, in order to gain AO5 marks, you must show that you understand this. This can be achieved by referring to critics, referring to productions or films, applying theory-based approaches (such as Marxist or feminist criticism) or by simply discussing a point from another angle.

Synopses

Before approaching this guide, students are expected to have read through both plays thoroughly. Nevertheless, these synopses are here to refresh your memory:

The Duchess of Malfi

The play is set in Italy, a Roman Catholic nation. Before the events of the play begin, the Duke of Amalfi has died, leaving his young wife, the Duchess, a widow. The Duchess' two brothers, the Cardinal and the Duke of Ferdinand, are corrupt and infamous individuals, who hope that their sister will never marry again.

The play opens with Antonio, the Duchess' steward, returning from France. He praises the virtuous French court; this provides an ironic contrast to the corrupt Italian court, which is riddled with flatterers and sycophants. Bosola, an agent of the Cardinal's, then enters the stage, having recently been released from the galleys. He performed the crime he was sent there for on behalf of the Cardinal.

Antonio tells his friend, Delio, that the two brothers are corrupt and sinful individuals, who conceal their crimes in order to preserve their reputations. Their sister, the Duchess, however, is fair, noble and intelligent.

Whilst visiting their sister, the brothers order and threaten the Duchess never to marry again. She assures them that she has no intention of doing so. Nevertheless, the brothers remain anxious, and so they employ Bosola to spy on her, under the pretence that they have selected him as the new manager of her horses.

After they leave, the Duchess informs the audience that she is going to defy her brothers by choosing a new husband. She inverts the traditional gender roles of the time by wooing Antonio, and they marry in secret.

Meanwhile, the Cardinal is having an affair with a married woman, named Julia.

After some time has passed, the Duchess is pregnant. Bosola discovers this (though he is not yet aware that Antonio is the father) and informs the brothers of their sister's disobedience. Ferdinand is incensed by the news, and the violence of his anger even shocks the Cardinal. Nevertheless, they decide to wait and discover who the father is before punishing the Duchess.

During this time, the Duchess and Antonio have more children. Ferdinand then decides to confront his sister, and acquires a key to her bedchamber. He enters her room and threatens her with a poniard (dagger), suggesting that she use it to kill herself. After he leaves, the Duchess plots to save

Antonio by pretending that he has been stealing from her, as this provides the pretext for firing him and thus getting him out of Amalfi. However, she makes a fatal mistake by confiding in Bosola, informing him that Antonio is her husband and the father of her children. She then plans to flee herself and join her family.

Bosola relays this information to the two brothers. As a result, the Cardinal has the family banished, whilst Ferdinand has the Duchess imprisoned in her home. Antonio and their eldest son, however, manage to flee to Milan.

After having the Duchess imprisoned in her estate, Ferdinand arranges for his sister to be tortured. He gives her a dead man's hand, for example, and pretends that it was Antonio's. Similarly, he reveals plaster-cast dummies resembling corpses, and claims that they are her dead husband and children. Finally, he arranges for "madfolk" from an asylum to be taken into the Duchess' room, who dance and sing around her. Despite these attempts, however, Ferdinand grows increasingly frustrated as the Duchess remains composed and endures the torture, unafraid. Eventually, Bosola is ordered to strangle the Duchess and her serving maid, Cariola.

After his sister's murder, Ferdinand is tortured by his guilty conscience, and he loses his mind. He attacks his own shadow, and howls like an animal. He is diagnosed with "lycanthropia" by a doctor; a disease which causes him to believe that he is a wolf. Bosola, too, laments over his actions, but he remains sane.

In Milan, Antonio (unaware of his wife's death) decides that he will attempt to remedy the situation by confronting the Cardinal. Meanwhile, the Cardinal orders

Bosola to murder Antonio. Bosola, however, is no longer willing to act as the agent of the corrupt brothers.

Julia, the Cardinal's mistress, sets eyes on Bosola and is smitten. Bosola uses this to manipulate her into trying to get the Cardinal to confess his part in the Duchess' murder. Julia agrees, and she attempts to entice the Cardinal's secret from him, whilst Bosola hides and eavesdrops. Eventually, the Cardinal confesses, but he instructs her to vow that she will never reveal his secret to anyone by kissing a Bible. The book, however, is poisoned, and Julia dies.

After this murder, Bosola reveals himself. He lies to the Cardinal, by pretending that he will murder Antonio in return for payment. In reality, Bosola hopes to save Antonio and murder the two brothers.

In the Cardinal's estate, the Cardinal instructs the sycophantic courtiers not to enter his room, even if they hear screaming and cries for help. Antonio sneaks into the palace, hoping to confront the Cardinal, unaware that Bosola is doing the same thing. The two meet in a dark corridor, and Bosola stabs Antonio, mistaking him for the Cardinal, and Antonio dies.

Plagued by yet more guilt, Bosola continues his search for the Cardinal. He finds and stabs him, and the courtiers – following their orders – do not come to help. Ferdinand then enters the room, and, in his madness, stabs both Bosola and the Cardinal. Bosola then stabs Ferdinand, and the three men die.

After this chaotic scene, Delio enters with Antonio's eldest son, and announces his intention to help the boy obtain his inheritance as his mother's heir.

A Streetcar Named Desire

Blanche DuBois, a former schoolteacher, arrives in New Orleans. She is standing outside an apartment building on a street called Elysian Fields, carrying luggage. She is looking for her sister, Stella, with whom she is hoping to stay for the foreseeable future. Blanche is shocked by, and snobbish about, her sister's new way of life; Stella and her husband, Stanley Kowalski, live in a small and shabby two-room apartment. Despite this superior attitude, however, Blanche is evidently anxious, and she helps herself to a drink of whiskey. She tells Stella that the home in which they grew up, Belle Reve, has been lost due to financial difficulties. Stanley returns home and meets Blanche, and she reveals, towards the end of their conversation, that she had been married when she was young, but her husband had died.

The next evening, Stella tells Stanley about the loss of Belle Reve, and he is suspicious that Blanche may have sold the estate and kept the profits for herself, rather than sharing them with her sister. He roots through her belongings. When Blanche enters the room, Stanley confronts her, demanding to see the documents concerning the loss of Belle Reve. When Blanche shows him the documents, Stanley realises that he was wrong. He tells Blanche that he it is his duty to be concerned about financial matters, because Stella is pregnant with their child. Blanche and Stella then go out for the evening.

Whilst Blanche and Stella are out, Stanley and three friends (Pablo, Steve and Mitch) are playing poker. Blanche notices that Mitch is more sensitive and gentle than the others, and the two have a conversation. Stanley, drunk,  becomes increasingly frustrated with Blanche and Stella, who he considers to be disrupting the game. He throws a radio out of the window and hits his wife, who retreats from him into the upstairs apartment (belonging to Steve and his wife, Eunice). From downstairs, Stanley calls for Stella to come back to him. Eventually she does so, and the couple embrace before returning to their apartment.

The following morning, Stella is cleaning the apartment after the poker night. Blanche is distressed by the events of the previous evening, and tries to convince Stella to leave Stanley and come away with her. Stella tells Blanche that she is being hysterical. Nevertheless, Blanche speaks increasingly critically of Stanley, and he overhears part of this criticism. When he enters the apartment, Stella greets him with an embrace.

Stanley questions Blanche about a disreputable hotel in Laurel (where Blanche was working as an English teacher) called the Flamingo. When he leaves, Blanche seeks assurance from Stella that nothing awful is known about her. Stella then leaves, and a young man comes by to collect subscriptions for a newspaper. Blanche flirts with him, before asking him to kiss her. After he leaves, Mitch arrives to take Blanche out on a date.

Blanche and Mitch return from their date, which has been unsuccessful. Blanche teases Mitch in French. When he tries to kiss her, she brushes him away, telling him that she has old fashioned ideals. By the end of the evening, Blanche opens up to Mitch by telling him about her former husband, Allan, who she discovered in bed with another man. After this discovery, Blanche, Allan and the other man went out dancing, pretending that nothing had happened. During the dance, Blanche told Allan that he disgusted her, and shortly afterwards he fled the room and shot himself. Mitch puts his arms around Blanche and tells her that they both need somebody.

In the next scene, it is Blanche's birthday, and she is singing in the bath, off stage. Stanley enters and tells Stella everything that he has learnt about Blanche's past: whilst living at Belle Reve, Blanche was promiscuous, sleeping with soldiers when they returned, drunk, to their barracks at night. After the loss of Belle Reve, she continued her promiscuous life at a cheap hotel, whilst also working as an English teacher. However, she lost her job after trying to seduce a seventeen-year-old student, after which she left Laurel to live with Stella and Stanley. As he recounts this story, Stella protests and tries to stop him, defending her sister. Stanley admits that he has told Mitch everything that he has discovered, which frustrates and saddens Stella. Blanche enters the room and can sense that something has happened.

Stella, Stanley and Blanche sit at the table and eat the birthday meal that Stella has prepared. Mitch is noticeably absent. Stella criticises Stanley's manners, and he responds by shouting at the two sisters and smashing his plate on the floor. He then gives Blanche a birthday present, which is a bus ticket back to Laurel. This distresses her, and she runs into the bathroom to vomit. Stella reacts angrily to this deliberate cruelty, before the baby moves in her stomach and she asks Stanley to take her to the hospital.

Blanche is alone in the house, and Mitch arrives, drunk. He criticises Blanche, and she tries to explain her behaviour as a means of surviving through the guilt and despair that has been plaguing her ever since the death of her husband. Mitch is not sympathetic, and he tries to rape her. Blanche cries out "Fire!", and he clumsily runs away.

Blanche is alone again in the apartment, and she dresses up in an evening gown. Stanley returns home from the hospital, drunk and happy after the birth of his child. Blanche tells him that she has been invited on a Caribbean cruise by a millionaire named Shep Huntleigh, who was an old admirer of hers. She also tells him that Mitch came by to apologise, but she turned him away. Stanley becomes increasingly aggressive, and tells Blanche that he knows that she is lying. Blanche becomes frightened, and tries to scare him away from her with a broken bottle. He disarms her, however, and carries her away to rape her.

A few weeks later, Stella is packing Blanche's trunk, whilst Stanley and his friends play poker. Blanche is in the bathroom, unaware that her sister is waiting for a doctor to arrive, who will take Blanche away to an institution for the mentally ill. Stella tells Eunice that she cannot believe

Blanche's accusation against Stanley and continue living with her husband. Blanche believes that she is waiting for the millionaire Shep Huntleigh to come and take her away, and is shocked by the arrival of the doctor and matron. The doctor treats her with courtesy, however, and she agrees to leave with him. Stella begins to cry as her sister is taken away. Stanley tries to comfort her, before beginning to open her blouse.

Addressing AO4

AO4 requires candidates to explore connections between *The Duchess of Malfi* and *A Streetcar Named Desire*. It is the <u>most important assessment objective</u> in this paper, because it is worth 20 marks. The other assessment objectives are worth 10 marks (see grid on pages 6 and 7). It is crucial, therefore, that you are consistently comparing the two plays.

This guide will take you through some of the key themes which are shared by both plays (see page 62 onwards). Looking at common themes will help you to draw further connections between the two plays.

<u>Here are some top tips to ensure that you are addressing AO4 as fully as possible:</u>

1) **Structure your essay around connections**. This is crucial; every paragraph in your essay should refer to <u>both plays</u>. Devoting a whole paragraph to one play, even if you make short, cursory references to the other within it, is a recipe for disaster.

Paragraph One – *The Duchess of Malfi*

Paragraph Two – *A Streetcar Named Desire*

Paragraph Three – *The Duchess of Malfi*

Paragraph Four – *A Streetcar Named Desire*

2) In order to structure your essay around connections, **the first sentence of every paragraph should present an idea which spans across both plays.**

These sentences could reflect on a key <u>similarity</u>; for example: *"Both plays suggest that losing possession of the mind is a fate worse than death."*

Alternatively, you could draw attention to a <u>contrast</u>; for example: *"Whilst Webster presents madness as a gruesome spectacle, Williams provides a more complex and subtle depiction of mental instability."*

What matters is that <u>both plays are being discussed from the very first line.</u> Try to avoid beginning with phrases such as, "In *A Streetcar Named Desire*…" or "In *The Duchess of Malfi*…." Instead, be comparative from the outset.

For more information on structuring paragraphs, go to page 148 ("Writing your Essay").

3) Use **comparative language**. This clearly shows an examiner that you are addressing AO4:

    a. Similarly…

b. By contrast...
c. <u>Both</u> Webster and Williams suggest that....
d. Likewise...
e. In contrast to this....
f. <u>Whilst</u> Webster does x, Williams does y....
g. Conversely...
h. Whereas....

4) Revise by comparing the two plays. Once you have read the plays, making notes as you read, ensure that your revision is comparative. One way in which you can do this is by making notes or mind maps on particular <u>themes</u>:

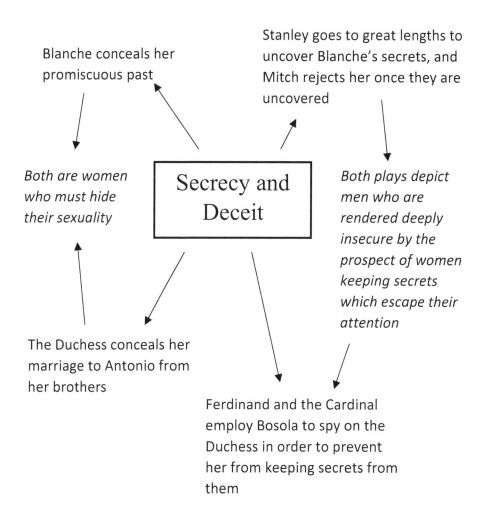

Blanche conceals her promiscuous past

Stanley goes to great lengths to uncover Blanche's secrets, and Mitch rejects her once they are uncovered

Both are women who must hide their sexuality

Secrecy and Deceit

Both plays depict men who are rendered deeply insecure by the prospect of women keeping secrets which escape their attention

The Duchess conceals her marriage to Antonio from her brothers

Ferdinand and the Cardinal employ Bosola to spy on the Duchess in order to prevent her from keeping secrets from them

This is a very small and rudimentary mind map (ideally you should be thinking of more ideas than this), but it serves to illustrate the point that you should always be drawing connections between the two plays during your revision.

The points in italics are ideas within the larger theme of "secrecy and deceit". These are the points on which the paragraphs of your essay could be based.

For more information on this theme, go to the "Secrecy and Deceit" section on page 99.

Addressing AO1

AO1 is part of every component in the WJEC Eduqas English Literature course. This is because it requires candidates to <u>write well</u>, and, in any essay, regardless of the subject matter, it is essential that you do this. That said, it is difficult to 'revise' for this assessment objective. Reading for pleasure, however, will help to improve your writing style. Moreover, this section will outline some of the criteria which is required for a good AO1 mark, and provide a few tips on how to ensure that your writing is sophisticated and formal in tone.

An Academic Register:

For a good AO1 mark, candidates are expected to adopt a "clear academic style and register". Clearly, this means that you must avoid colloquial and informal terms. Here are some other points to bear in mind:

1) <u>Avoid using the first person pronoun</u>. Phrases such as "I think…" or "In my opinion…" establish a personal tone. In order to adopt an "academic register", you must be objective and analytical.

2) <u>Refer to the plays as plays</u>. This may seem like an obvious point, but many candidates use phrases

such as "in the book" or terms such as "narrative" or "the reader". It is always important to bear in mind that both Webster and Williams were envisaging the performance of their work as they wrote; they did not intend for their material to be read.

3) <u>Avoid contractions</u>, such as "wouldn't", "can't" or "shouldn't". Instead, write "would not", "cannot" or "should not".

4) When you first refer to a playwright in an introduction, it is acceptable to use their full name. After this, use only their <u>surnames</u>: Webster and Williams.

5) Plays should always be referred to *in italics*. If you handwrite examinations, you can indicate this by underlining the titles of the plays, like so: <u>The Duchess of Malfi</u>.

6) When you are referring to a technique used by a playwright, make sure that you are writing in the <u>present tense</u>. For example, write "Williams **uses** ominous imagery to foreshadow the impending rape", rather than "Williams used ominous imagery...."

Spelling, Grammar and Punctuation:

It is important that you avoid making spelling, punctuation and grammatical errors which might irritate an English Literature examiner. Of course, this is easier said than done when you are writing under examination conditions. This is why time management is so crucial; try to leave yourself two minutes at the end of the exam to read over your essay and ensure that you fix any accidental mistakes.

Terminology:

Meeting AO1 also involves using literary terminology. This means that you must make references to the **similes**, **metaphors**, **personification** et cetera which are being employed by the playwright to achieve a certain effect. However, it is vital that you use these terms relevantly, assessing their purpose and effect. English literature examiners are always frustrated by "labelling". This is when you identify a simile, for example, but do not analyse its effect. Identifying literary terms for its own sake will never gain you any credit at A-level. Similarly, it is important that you do not 'overuse' terminology. Whilst it can help you to make your analysis more specific, it should be used sparingly and thoughtfully.

Organisation:

There are also AO1 marks available for organising your essay effectively and sensibly. Whilst you do not need to write a detailed plan during the examination (unless you are a very fast writer, you do not have the time), it is important that you jot down the key points you want to discuss in each paragraph, and consider the best way in which to organise them.

In order to clearly show evidence of organisation in your essay, try to link the first sentence of your paragraph with the point you have made in the paragraph that precedes it. Connectives – such as, "However", "Moreover" or "Similarly" – will help you to do this.

Addressing AO2

AO2 is literary analysis, and it is included in every paper of your English Literature A-Level. In order to achieve the highest marks in this assessment objective, the exam board requires candidates to demonstrate "perceptive, sophisticated analysis and evaluation of writers' use of <u>language</u> and <u>dramatic techniques</u> to create meaning." This means that you must consider the effect of exits, entrances, costume and other theatrical features as well as **dialogue**.

There is clearly some overlap with AO1 here: if you are writing fluently, your analysis will be clearer and appear more sophisticated. Remember to be aware of 'labelling' when it comes to using literary and dramatic terminology: the exam board specifically states that you must demonstrate how Webster and Williams use techniques "to create meaning". You must assess <u>the effect</u> of techniques, rather than simply identifying them.

Of course, to analyse the playwrights' use of language well, you must have learnt some quotations from the plays, because you will <u>not</u> have copies of the texts with you in the exam. Indeed, making "confident" and "secure" references to the text is required for the highest AO2 marks. In order to ensure that you remember quotations correctly, use short, succinct ones which clearly illustrate your point. Where appropriate, use **ellipses** in square brackets (like so: [...]) to indicate that you are omitting part of a quotation, for example:

Ferdinand and the Cardinal are likened to "plum trees that grow crooked over standing pools [...] none but crows, pies and caterpillars feed on them."

If you want to change part of the original text, use <u>square brackets</u>, like so:

Blanche acknowledges that she has "got to be good and keep [her] hands off children."

AO2 also requires candidates to evaluate underlying, or implicit, meanings. One way in which this can be achieved is by analysing **motifs** and **symbols**. This is because a symbol, by its very nature, is something which bears an underlying or alternative meaning.

Take a moment to read through the next few pages, which discuss some of the key motifs and symbols in both plays.

Disease

The Duchess of Malfi

Images of disease, pollution and sickness are introduced from the very outset of the play. In Act 1 scene i, Webster likens "a prince's court" to a "common fountain":

"...if't chance some cursed example poison't near the head,

Death and diseases through the whole land spread."

This motif persists throughout the play. Bosola likens the courtiers to "crows, pies and caterpillars", for example, and reflects on the "rotten" state of mankind. Similarly, the Duchess' pregnancy is presented as a kind of sickness: "she pukes, her stomach seethes..." Ferdinand, meanwhile, declares that his sister must be killed "to purge infected blood", and, after she has been murdered, he suffers from the "very pestilent disease" of "lycanthropia", which causes him to believe that he is a wolf.

This **lexical field** of disease perhaps reinforces the notion that the Italian court has been poisoned "near the head", and thus, by repeatedly alluding to sickness and corruption, the audience are given the impression that this disease has "spread" everywhere.

The Streetcar

A Streetcar Named Desire

In Scene IV, Blanche tells Stella that a streetcar named Desire "brought" her to Elysian Fields. This is a real streetcar line in New Orleans; it caught Williams' attention when he was living in the city in 1946.

The streetcar named desire is a symbol for desire. Blanche's sexual liaisons force her out of Laurel and leave her with nowhere to go other than the home of her sister and brother-in-law. Like a streetcar, they drive her to this destination. Blanche herself has no control; she is only a passenger.

The play is named after this symbol because it explores the power of sexual passion over the lives of human beings. Stella, for example, abandons her sister as a result of it. Desire is the driving force behind the actions and decisions of the characters, and this, Williams suggests, leads to ruin.

Ferdinand's Poniard:

The Duchess of Malfi

After ordering the Duchess never to marry again, Ferdinand threatens her with a weapon: "This was my father's poniard…" It has been suggested that this phallic image expresses Ferdinand's incestuous feelings for his sister. In addition, it could also be seen as a symbol of patriarchal power: like patriarchal power, it has been handed down to him after the death of his father. Ferdinand, therefore, is attempting to use this tool to control his sister, and he does so again in Act III scene ii. It is notable, however, that the Duchess dies not by this weapon but by strangling. Is Webster suggesting that Ferdinand never truly gets the better of his sister? The Duchess' heroic death, and Ferdinand's subsequent madness, might be used to support this notion.

Bathing

A Streetcar Named Desire

To Stanley's frustration, Blanche is frequently bathing in this play. This underscores her guilt and self-loathing; she wants to 'cleanse' herself of her past mistakes. Indeed, in order to be eligible for marriage (which she must be, if she is to achieve the financial security she requires to survive), Blanche must have a 'clean' reputation. Ultimately, however, Blanche's bathing is futile; as Mitch tells her in Scene IX, she is "not clean enough" to be his wife.

Light and the Paper Lantern

A Streetcar Named Desire

Throughout *A Streetcar Named Desire*, Blanche tries to avoid light. When she first arrives in Elysian Fields, she orders Stella to turn off the light, telling her that she "won't be looked at in this merciless glare!" Williams reinforces this idea later, when he has Blanche tell Mitch that she "can't stand a naked lightbulb". On a literal level, this is because she does not want others to see her face – "daylight never exposed so total a ruin", as she tells Stella. Towards the end of the play, Mitch holds Blanche under the bulb so he can confirm his suspicion that she's "older than what [he] thought".

Light serves a deeper purpose than this, however. It can be seen to represent truth; like the truth, light is illuminating. Blanche, however, "doesn't want realism": "I don't tell the truth, I tell what *ought* to be the truth". She is desperate to avoid the truth of her past by constructing fictions and telling lies. This notion is reinforced by the popular ballad, "It's only a Paper Moon", which she sings in the bath: "It wouldn't be make-believe if you believed in me!" In Blanche's view, telling lies is not deceitful or harmful, but "magic". It allows her to believe in a happier reality.

As a result, Blanche constructs a **façade**. This is also to protect herself; in the early twentieth century, unmarried woman were at risk of becoming destitute as they aged, unless they had wealthier relatives to support them. Blanche's promiscuous history, however, makes marriage an unlikely prospect, given the cruel gender-based double standards of the time. Thus, Blanche must pretend that she is a virgin in order to survive.

In Scene III, Blanche asks Mitch to hang up an "adorable little coloured paper lantern" in order to cover the lightbulb. If we are viewing light as a symbol for truth in the play, then the paper lantern is obscuring and concealing truth; it serves to represent Blanche's façade. It is interesting, therefore, that Mitch tears down the paper lantern in Scene IX. This shows us that Blanche's lies and fabrications have now been fully destroyed; after discovering her promiscuous past, they are no longer believed in by anyone. This has ruined her marriage prospects, which in turn has destroyed her.

The Varsouviana Polka

A Streetcar Named Desire

As Blanche tells Mitch in Scene VI, she and her late husband, Allan Grey, danced the Varsouviana after she found him in bed with another man ("we pretended that nothing had been discovered"). During this dance, Blanche told Allan that he "disgust[s]" her, and shortly after this he committed suicide. Blanche, therefore, associates the music with her husband and his death, and it plays whenever she is reminded of him. None of the other characters hear this; it plays only in her mind. The Polka, therefore, reminds the audience that Blanche is haunted by tragic memories, and reinforces her mental fragility. As Mitch insensitively comments in Scene IX, she is "boxed out" of her own mind.

The Poisoned Bible

The Duchess of Malfi

In Act V scene ii, Bosola exploits Julia's lust for him by encouraging her to discover the cause of the Cardinal's "wondrous melancholy". Julia is successful in this: the Cardinal confesses to her that the Duchess and her children were murdered "by [his] appointment". However, he has her swear on a Bible that she will not reveal this to anyone, and orders her to kiss the book. Unaware that it is poisoned, Julia does so, and dies.

The Bible is, of course, a holy book, and the Cardinal, a religious figure, is behaving sacrilegiously by soaking it in poison and using it as a murder weapon. Throughout the play, he exploits his position and power within the church for his own corrupt purposes; he uses religion as an instrument to inflict harm upon others. A poisoned Bible, therefore, is an apt weapon, and a clear symbol of this abuse of power.

Remember that AO4 (comparison) is the most heavily weighted assessment objective. Can you think of any symbols which are shared by both plays? Here are a couple of ideas:

Ominous Imagery

Both playwrights cultivate an atmosphere of foreboding from the outset, which serves to **foreshadow** the plays' tragic conclusions. One way in which they achieve this is through their use of portentous symbols. Consider the following:

- Antonio's handkerchief is bloodied by a nosebleed. The blood blots out his initials, foreshadowing his death.
- On her journey to Elysian Fields, Blanche transfers from a streetcar named Desire to a streetcar named Cemeteries.
- Before her death, Ferdinand has the executioners deliver a coffin to his sister. He also uses a dead man's hand and models of Antonio and the children to distress her.
- In Scene IX, a Mexican flower seller enters the stage, selling flowers for the dead. In the next scene, "lurid shadows" and "inhuman voices" foreshadow the impending violence.

Animal Imagery

In both plays, human beings are depicted as greedy, selfish, violent and cruel. In addition, both present characters who are led by their sexual impulses. With this in mind, consider why Webster and Williams employ images and metaphors relating to animals throughout their plays. Below are a few examples; see if you can find any more.

- Stanley is described as possessing "the power and pride of a richly feathered male bird among his hens".
- The Cardinal likens Julia to a bird which he has tamed and trained: "I have taken you off your melancholy perch, bore you upon my fist, and showed you game..." She is also compared to a "tame elephant".
- In Scene III, Stella and Stanley come together with "low animal moans".
- Bosola refers to himself as Ferdinand's "creature".
- In Scene IV, Blanche exclaims that Stanley is "like an animal" with "animal habits". She describes him as "bestial" and "ape-like".
- Ferdinand's "lycanthropia" causes him to believe that he is a wolf.
- Before Stanley attacks Blanche in Scene X, the audience hear "inhuman jungle voices rise up."

Addressing AO3

AO3 requires students to use their contextual knowledge in order to enhance their analysis of the plays. The specification clearly states that candidates can refer to the context in which the plays were <u>written</u> as well as the context in which they were <u>received</u>.

Context in which a play was written:

John Webster wrote the *Duchess of Malfi* whilst James I - whose court was infamous for its favouritism and vice - was on the throne. The presentation of corrupt individuals within the play is perhaps indirect criticism of this.

Context in which a play was received:

In the first stage production of *A Streetcar Named Desire*, the audience cheered when Stanley carried Blanche away to rape her. This shows that the gender-based double standards which destroy Blanche in the play were still very much alive in the real world.

Both are equally valid and useful. The key point to take away is that you must refer to context in a <u>relevant</u> manner. The lowest AO3 marks (1-2 out of 10) are given to students who merely "describe" the wider context, whilst the highest marks are awarded to candidates who are "productive" in their use of contextual information. This means that you must use context to further your analysis; it should not be an irrelevant sentence which is thrown into a paragraph in order to 'tick the AO3 box'.

Have a look at the difference between candidates A and B:

Candidate A: The antimasque is a gruesome parody of the court masque, a form of entertainment in the Renaissance. This courtly entertainment developed in Italy, and thrived in the sixteenth and early seventeenth centuries. It involved singing, dancing and the wearing of masks; often the masquers were courtiers.

Candidate B: The antimasque is a gruesome parody of the court masque, a form of entertainment in the Renaissance. The horror of the scene may well have resonated more with a contemporary audience, because they would have seen it as subverting a traditionally pleasant activity, with which they were familiar, into a horrific spectacle.

Both candidates will gain <u>some</u> AO3 credit, but Candidate B's mark will be much higher, because the contextual information is relevant and useful. Candidate B has used this information to further their literary analysis, whilst Candidate's A work could be mistaken for an extract from a history essay.

It is vital that your work remains a literary essay. This is the danger with AO3: though it is crucial that you address it, diverging from the plays too much will cost you marks in the other AOs, which, collectively (or individually in the case of AO4), are worth far more marks.

Revising Context:

Contextual information is one of those things which you simply have to learn. You can ensure that you use it relevantly by always relating it to the plays and how it might impact our – or the original audience's – interpretation of it. This guide will help with this by drawing relevant context into discussions of key themes (see page 62 onwards).

Nevertheless, it is important to have some of the basic context 'under your belt' before we can take the discussion further: take a moment to read through the next few pages.

1) *The Duchess of Malfi*: Source Material

The basic plot of Webster's play was inspired by **William Painter's "Duchess of Malfy"**, which appears in his work *The Palace of Pleasure* (c.1567). Painter's work is an account (though not the first) of real events: The Duchess of Amalfi, Giovanna d'Aragona, was born in 1478. She was widowed before she remarried Antonio Bologna. For this, her two brothers decreed her murder.

Painter presents a strikingly unflattering image of the Duchess. She is described as a "foolish woman" who married to "glut her own libidinous appetite". This, clearly, is very different from Webster's heroic figure ("a behaviour so noble as gives a majesty to adversity"). If Webster is refusing to conform to the misogynistic foundations laid out by Painter, what does this suggest about his sympathies for the Duchess' situation? Does it enable us to refer to him as a proto-feminist? Answering these questions will ensure that your use of context is relevant.

2) *A Streetcar Named Desire*: The American Civil War

The American Civil War began in 1861, after several southern American states seceded from the union and formed the Confederate States of America. Tensions between the north and south existed for a variety of reasons, but a key one was the issue of slavery. The north regarded slavery as a moral evil, whilst the south relied on it in order to maintain the plantations on which their prosperity depended. President Abraham Lincoln denounced the Confederate States as rebels, and, as more southern states began to break away, war broke out.

The war ended in 1865, when the Confederate States surrendered. After this, the prosperity of the South was in decline. In the 20th century, the Civil War and the lost southern way of life were often romanticised in literature and the arts. Margaret Mitchell's novel *Gone with the Wind* is a famous example of this.

The decline of the south is fundamental to the basic plot of *A Streetcar Named Desire*: the Dubois family estate, Belle Reve, has been lost. The fact that Stella, who was part of the wealthy, landowning Dubois family, has married Stanley, a working-class man, serves to illustrate the extent to which the social fabric in America has been altered by 1947 – the year in which the play is set.

A famous reading of the play is to interpret Blanche as a **personification** of the "Old South", and to see Stanley as an embodiment of the industrial "New America", which had emerged as a world power after the Second World War. The power struggle between the two characters serves to symbolise the conflict between the dying past and the emerging future, and Stanley's victory over Blanche suggests that, for better or for worse, the "Old South" is now a relic of the past.

Alternatively, it could be argued that Williams suggests that these two ways of life have merged together, symbolised by the birth of Stella and Stanley's baby boy. Either way, the ending of the play is bleak. Is it <u>wholly without</u> optimism for the future?

Names are always significant in this play, and note the name of the Dubois family estate: Belle Reve. This means 'beautiful dream' in French. Is Williams being nostalgic here, by mourning the loss of a 'beautiful' past? Or is he implying that, like a dream, this beauty was only illusory, and never really existed at all?

3) *The Duchess of Malfi*: Revenge

The Duchess of Malfi is a **revenge tragedy**. This genre was very popular in English theatres during the late 16th and 17th centuries. As its name suggests, revenge tragedies are plays which are driven by the **protagonist**'s desire to take revenge for an atrocity committed by another character, the **antagonist**.

In *The Duchess of Malfi*, several revenge plots are set into motion. Initially, Ferdinand and the Cardinal seek revenge on the Duchess and Antonio for their marriage. After this, Bosola seeks to punish the Cardinal for exploiting him.

Inspired by the works of Roman philosopher and playwright Seneca, revenge tragedies are characterised by violent murders and bloody horrors. *The Duchess of Malfi* certainly conforms to this tradition: consider the dead man's hand which is used to torture the Duchess, the wax figures of Antonio and the children, the strangling of the Duchess of Cariola, and the multiple murders which conclude the play.

Webster's plays are often criticised for being gratuitously violent and dismissed as mere sensationalism. To what extent would you agree with this view, having read *The Duchess of Malfi*? Theatre critic Michael Bilington suggests that, whilst the play is bloody, this bloodiness serves a deeper purpose: it underscores the idea that "life is unstable, accidental, perhaps ultimately meaningless: 'a general mist of error'".

4) *A Streetcar Named Desire*: Mental Illness

Williams' sister, Rose, was given a bilateral prefrontal lobotomy (part of her brain was removed) as a treatment for mental illness. She was institutionalised for much of her life, and Williams himself suffered from a nervous breakdown at the age of twenty-four. His experience with mental illness, therefore, perhaps accounts for the subtle and complex depiction of it in *A Streetcar Named Desire*.

Rose never recovered from the lobotomy, and Williams admitted to being plagued by guilt as a result of his not preventing it. Perhaps Stella's cruel betrayal of her sister at the end of the play is an expression of Williams' own sense of guilt.

5) *The Duchess of Malfi*: Italy

In the late 16th and early 17th century, it was common for English playwrights to set their plays in foreign locations. They were relatively unique in this respect; contemporary theatres in European countries tended to focus on their own cultures and history.

Italy was a common choice; just take a look at a handful of Shakespeare's plays: *Romeo and Juliet*, *Othello*, *The Taming of the Shrew*, *The Merchant of Venice*. One reason for this is that the sources from which English playwrights took their stories already had an Italian setting. This was the case for Webster, since the real events which inspired William Painter's "Duchess of Malfy" did indeed occur in Italy.

Nevertheless, the play's first audiences in the 17th century would probably have considered Italy to be a very fitting setting, because many associated it with corruption and vice. Many would have been aware, for example, of the notorious Italian political theorist Niccolo Machiavelli, who, in his work *The Prince* (published in 1532, nearly a century before *The Duchess of Malfi*), suggests that a successful nation requires a strong ruler who can ensure the safety and prosperity of his people, and that it was acceptable to employ "some criminal or nefarious method" in order to achieve these aims. Some interesting parallels could be drawn between this philosophy and the criminal activities of the powerful characters in the play.

In addition to the legacy of Machiavelli, religious prejudice was also a cause of Italy's corrupt reputation amongst the English. Italy was home to the Pope, the centre of Catholic authority, whilst England was a Protestant nation. The presentation of the Cardinal, who wields a lot of power within the Catholic church, as a corrupt and malevolent villain, perhaps reflects the anti-Catholic sentiments of the time.

The Italian setting did not only enable Webster to criticise foreigners, however; it also allowed him to attack his own government, without fear of persecution. The corruption of the Italian court in the play, therefore, could be seen as indirect criticism of the court of James I, who notoriously granted privileges and wealth to his favourite courtiers (hence the references to "flatt'ring sycophants" and "panders" at the beginning of the play).

6) *A Streetcar Named Desire*: Homosexuality

For the majority of Williams' life, **homosexuality was illegal**, and so he, like Blanche, was forced to conceal his sexuality. It is alleged by some critics that Williams loathed himself for his homosexuality, and the debate surrounding gay rights that was beginning to emerge at this time never appears as a major theme in his works. Nevertheless, it has been claimed, to borrow Patricia Hern and Michael Hooper's words, that Blanche is a kind of "'cover' for a male character, a homosexual, given a female mask by Williams so as to avoid having to confront his own feelings about himself." Blanche is mocked by Stanley for her effeminate behaviour (just as Williams was derided by his father, who used to call him "Miss Nancy") and she is forced to lie about herself to everyone, including her own sister, in order to survive.

7) *The Duchess of Malfi*: Corruption

The mediaeval theory of microcosm and macrocosm
was still influential in Webster's time. This theory held
that a monarch's physical and emotional state was
representative of the country as a whole; the king was
the "head", metaphorically, of the state's "body". This
logic maintained that if the king was physically weak,
the nation would be as well. Similarly, if the king was
morally corrupt, there would be evidence of
degeneration in the country. This idea perhaps
inspired the motif of disease which persists
throughout the play (see page 29), as well as the
simile which launches the opening scene: "a prince's
court is like a common fountain..."

8) *A Streetcar Named Desire*: Working Titles

The title of Williams' play is so striking and
memorable that it is difficult, today, to imagine it
being called anything else. It is important, however, to
remember that Williams, like all writers, wrote drafts
and drafts, analysing and re-assessing, before he came
to his final manuscript. The play was initially set in
Chicago, for example, and then Atlanta in Georgia,
before he finally settled on New Orleans.

Williams tested several titles before choosing *A
Streetcar Named Desire*. *The Poker Night*, *The Primary
Colours*, *The Moth* and *Blanche's Chair in The Moon*

were all working titles. By looking at these titles, we can surmise the elements of the play that Williams felt were most important. *The Primary Colours* and *The Poker Night*, for example, perhaps attract attention towards the male characters, and the play's presentation of masculinity. *The Poker Night* also bears connotations of competition, which perhaps reflects the power struggle between Stanley and Blanche.

By contrast, *The Moth* and *Blanche's Chair in The Moon* encourage us to focus on Blanche. The first reinforces the idea of fatal attraction (like a moth drawn to a bulb, Blanche's sexual desire leads to her ruin), whilst the second – which perhaps brings to mind the ballad "It's only a Paper Moon", which Blanche sings in Scene VII - emphasises the theme of self-delusion.

It is interesting, too, to consider why Williams chose to move away from these options and settle on *A Streetcar Named Desire* instead. As we mentioned on page 30, this was a real streetcar line in New Orleans, which caught Williams' attention when he was living in the city in 1946:

"Down this street, running on the same tracks, are two streetcars, one named Desire, the other Cemetery. Their indiscourageable progress up and down Royal struck me as having some symbolic bearing of a broad nature... And that's how I got the title."

One interesting feature of this new title is that it serves to disempower Blanche. Whilst *The Moth* (with the more self-confident definite article, "The") and *Blanche's Chair in The Moon* (in which she is the eponymous heroine) placed Blanche at the centre of the story, *A Streetcar Named Desire* replaces her with a metaphor for desire – the force that will destroy her.

Addressing AO5

Assessment Objective 5 requires candidates to assess the two plays from <u>different critical angles</u>. It expects students to understand that there is never one way in which a text can be understood. For the highest marks in this area, you should not only embed other critical viewpoints, but <u>assess</u> the extent to which you regard them as valid.

<u>There are a variety of ways in which candidates can address AO5:</u>

1) Quoting a critic directly:

For example: *Michael Billington suggests that Blanche deceives others "as a protection against solitude and desperation".*

Paraphrasing is also acceptable: *Michael Billington suggests that Blanche's deceit is a protective measure, which she uses to shield herself from despair.*

Referring to a critic is perhaps the clearest way to show an examiner that you are aware of and interested in readings of the play beyond your own. Thus, whilst learning critical quotations, on top of quotations from the texts themselves, can appear a daunting task, **do not** decide to disregard this. Though there is no such thing as a perfect "checklist" for English Literature – and you must ensure that your **allusions** to critics are made in a <u>relevant</u> manner – attempt to make at least <u>two references to critical material in your essay</u>. Always referring to critics in practice essays, furthermore, will help you to remember them.

The best way to learn critical quotations is, simply, to devote part of your revision time to reading critical material. Here are a few places to start you off if you are at a loss:

- Read the introductions to your own copies of the plays.

- The British Library have produced some interesting articles on *The Duchess of Malfi* which you can access for free. Just type "The British Library Duchess of Malfi" into a search engine; it should be the first option to come up.

- The English and Media Centre's magazine (*E-magazine*) is excellent, and has produced several articles on both *The Duchess of Malfi* and

A Streetcar Named Desire, as well as many other texts in the WJEC Eduqas English literature course. You will have to pay a subscription to access it *(if you are considering reading English at university, this subscription is definitely worthwhile anyway).*

- The Open University have a free course available on Acts I and II of *The Duchess of Malfi*. Again, just type "Open University Duchess of Malfi" into a search engine; it should be easy to find.

This guide will also refer to relevant critical quotations in discussions of key themes.

2) Theory-based approaches:

It is also possible to assess alternative readings by taking a theory-based approach. However, it is important, particularly when discussing *The Duchess of Malfi*, to remember that many of these literary theories came into existence after a play was written. It is **anachronistic**, therefore, to refer to John Webster as a "feminist" or a "Marxist", since feminism and Marxism did not exist when Webster was writing. However, it is possible to refer to Webster as a "proto-feminist", if you agree with the idea that *The Duchess of Malfi* espouses feminist values (a point which we will discuss further on page 65).

It is also important to use <u>tentative language</u> when you refer to a theory, such as "a psychoanalytic reading *might* suggest…" (as opposed to, "a psychoanalytic reading *would* suggest…"). This is because a theory will never provide a single response to a text; different feminist critics, for example, may come to different opinions. By applying a theory tentatively, you are showing an examiner that you understand that this is only one way in which the theory can be applied.

<u>Here are some theories for you to consider:</u>

Feminist Criticism: Broadly speaking, feminism is the belief that men and women should have equal rights and opportunities. It rejects the idea that one sex is inherently superior to the other.

Feminist literary criticism approaches literature by applying the ideas and principles of feminism. A feminist critic might look at how a text has been shaped or influenced by patriarchal attitudes: for example, are the female characters being presented as objects from a male perspective? If the female characters assert their independence or rights, are they demonised or ridiculed? You might have heard of the **Madonna-Whore Complex**: this is when a writer depicts only two kinds of female character – saintly, obedient "Madonnas", or morally corrupt, licentious "Whores". Is there evidence of this within a text?

Conversely, a feminist critic might also consider whether a writer is attempting to challenge or undercut patriarchal attitudes in their work. This approach might be used to challenge the male-dominated **canon** and investigate whether female writers, who were perhaps popular in their time, have been excluded from it on account of their sex.

An interesting aspect of *The Duchess of Malfi* and *A Streetcar Named Desire* is that, in both cases, it is ambiguous as to whether the playwrights are criticising or championing the rights of their female **protagonists**. Does Webster suggest that the Duchess is right to assert her independence? If so, why is she punished? Is Williams critical of Blanche's behaviour, or is he in fact criticising the society and double standards which destroy her?

Marxist Criticism: Marxist critics consider how power is gained, shared and maintained in a text. The theory examines how socio-economic conditions influence the actions, personality and behaviour of the characters, and ponders whether class struggles are at the root of the tensions between them.

As we mentioned in the discussion of the American Civil War on page 40, a Marxist critic may well approach *A Streetcar Named Desire* by viewing Blanche as the personification of the **bourgeois**, slave-owning "Old South", and argue that, in her power struggle with Stanley, she is attempting to prevent the rise of the new American urban **proletariat**.

Additionally, a Marxist reading of *The Duchess of Malfi* might attract sympathy for characters such as Bosola, suggesting that he has little choice – given the social paradigm in which the play is set – but to obey his powerful masters and commit acts of great evil. After all, when he finds the courage to disobey them, he dies.

Psychoanalytic Criticism: Founder of psychoanalysis Sigmund Freud suggested that our thoughts, actions, feelings and behaviour are informed not only by the conscious part of the mind, but by the subconscious. This part of the psyche consists of repressed desires and forgotten memories.

A psychoanalytic reading of a text might choose to explore the psychology of its characters, and how this informs their actions. Thus, a reading of this kind might suggest that Ferdinand has repressed incestuous feelings for his sister, and explore how these effect the action in the play.

Alternatively, a psychoanalytic critic might consider the psychology of the playwrights themselves, and how this influences the text. This approach might consider how Williams' homosexuality, self-loathing and fear of death shape the events of *A Streetcar Named Desire*, for example.

New Historicism: This approach considers the context in which a play was written, examining how the text reflects, or is shaped by, this context. This theory also suggests that we can learn more about the concerns of a time by reading and studying the literature that was produced during it.

In terms of *The Duchess of Malfi*, therefore, we might consider the favouritism and corruption in the court of James I, as well as contemporary attitudes towards Italy and Catholicism. In the case of *A Streetcar Named Desire*, meanwhile, we might examine attitudes towards women and sexuality in the 1940s, the decline of the "Old South" and the emergence of the United States as a world power following the Second World War. Clearly, New Historicism relies on being familiar with contextual material, so have a look at the "Addressing AO3" section for more detailed information.

3) Alternative Readings and Answering the Question:

Of course, it is possible to consider alternative readings yourself, without referring to a particular critic or theory (though explicitly naming a critic or theory will ensure that the examiner can clearly identify AO5 material in your work). For example, is Bosola a villain or a victim? Is Blanche a deceitful egotist or a helpless woman? Is order restored at the end of both plays, or are we left with a sense of chaos and despair? Using evidence from the text to weigh up both points-of-view demonstrates an awareness of the fact that there are alternative ways in which the texts and their characters can be interpreted and understood.

In addition, there are also AO5 marks available for maintaining a focus on the question. This is because making a convincing argument, which comes to a balanced and sophisticated conclusion, requires you to look at the argument from both sides and consider alternative points-of-view.

Please note, however, that both answering the question and considering alternative readings yourself should be done alongside referring to critics, not on its own.

4) Referencing Productions and Films:

When an actor plays a role, he or she is interpreting a script. Similarly, directors must interpret a playwright's work when they stage a film or a play. Thus, it is possible to address AO5 by referencing productions and films.

Watching productions and films will also help you learn quotations from the plays, and to better visualise the plays as a performance. As we mentioned in the "Addressing AO1" section: the plays were written to be performed, not read.

Indeed, watching a play is a different experience from reading a play, and this could serve to alter your view of the text. Roger Boxhill, for example, suggests that those who read *A Streetcar Named Desire* favour Blanche and demonise Stanley, whilst audiences (certainly at the beginning) favour Stanley. He attributes this partly to humour. On the stage, an audience might overlook the subtle indications of Blanche's mental instability (they cannot, after all, read Williams' intricate and detailed stage directions). Stanley's jokes, meanwhile, are perhaps more likely to have an impact in the environment of a theatre. The extent to which we sympathise with these characters has a deeply significant impact on the way in which we view the play as a whole – so do try and see a stage production if you can.

Of course, films are more readily available, if seeing a performance is not an option. Most of the original film of *A Streetcar Named Desire*, directed by Elia Kazan, is available on YouTube. If you can, try and see another production too – such as John Erman's 1984 adaptation of the play. Compare the two and consider the choices made by both directors.

<u>Here are some points and questions to consider about
these productions:</u>

- Elia Kazan wrote, in his private director's notebook,
  that "Blanche is dangerous. She is destructive",
  describing her as "a phony, corrupt, sick, destructive
  woman". To what extent do you think that Blanche
  conforms to this description in Kazan's film?

- In Erman's film, Blanche is presented as mentally
  unstable from the very outset, whilst, in Kazan's film,
  we see a more gradual decline into madness. Which
  do you think is the more powerful? Which
  interpretation is best supported by the text? Use
  quotations to support your answer.

- Think about the dramatic techniques used by the
  directors, and the opportunities offered by film as a
  medium. At the end of Erman's film, for example,
  voiceover and echo are used to emphasise Blanche's
  disturbed mental state.

- Before Kazan's film could be released, it was subject
  to censorship by the Production Code Administration,
  headed by Joseph Breen. They argued that Stanley
  ought to be punished for his actions. The film ends,
  therefore, not with Stella and Stanley embracing (as
  they are in the play), but with Stella running away
  from her husband with her child in her arms, to whom
  she promises that they will never return home. What

is the effect of changing the plot in this way? Is it credible, given Stella's behaviour and feelings earlier in the film?

- Consider the ways in which the directors choose to use Williams' motifs and symbols. At the end of Erman's film, Stanley mockingly asks Blanche if she wants to take the paper lantern with her to the mental institution, before dropping it on the floor, just out of her grasp. Later, when the matron is violently pinning Blanche to the floor, Blanche attempts to reach for the lantern, but cannot grasp it. Have a look at the discussion of the symbolism surrounding the paper lantern on page 32 – what do you think Erman is trying to suggest here?

It is a little harder to get hold of copies of films for *The Duchess of Malfi*. Though some are available on Amazon, these tend to be quite expensive. Nevertheless, it's always worth visiting your local library to see if they have a copy of a production which you could borrow.

Moreover, some of the Globe's 2014 production of *The Duchess of Malfi*, directed by Dominic Dromgoole and starring Gemma Arterton as the Duchess, is available on YouTube. This is a very interesting production; as we will mention later in the "Family Relationships" section on page 128, Dromgoole takes the view that Ferdinand – played by

David Dawson – has incestuous feelings for his sister. Theatre critic Michael Billington suggests that, "it is David Dawson as Ferdinand who really steals the show. From the start there is something clearly amiss with this tense, edgy, lank-locked Duke. He is palpably a victim of thwarted incest as you see when he feverishly imagines his twin sister in the act of love with 'some strong-thighed bargeman'."

Even if you are unable to see full productions, reading reviews by critics is a good way to learn of interesting interpretations, ideas and techniques used by directors and actors, which you can potentially discuss in an essay. Billington's review is available in full on the Guardian's website.

Something to consider:

It is possible to evaluate a director's interpretation of the text by considering the parts of the play that they chose to cut, as well as what they do with the parts that they include. For example, Dromgoole excludes the interaction between Bosola and the Old Lady in Act 2 scene i. Why do you think he made this decision? In your opinion, does this alter our impression of the play as a whole? Is something lost?

Key Themes

In this section we'll discuss some of the key common themes between the two plays, on which you could be asked a question.

Women and Gender

Perhaps one of the strongest connections between these plays is that they both have female protagonists who are the victims of male oppression and abuse.

<u>Consider the following questions...</u>

How far would you agree with the view that, "women are entirely powerless" in *The Duchess of Malfi* and *A Streetcar Named Desire*?

To what extent do you agree with the idea that, in *The Duchess of Malfi* and *A Streetcar Named Desire*, "Webster and Williams are critical of women for transgressing social norms"?

"Though we can sympathise, the audience cannot respect Blanche and the Duchess." In light of this view, explore connections between *The Duchess of Malfi* and *A Streetcar Named Desire*.

"Webster and Williams present female sexuality as a very frightening and destructive phenomenon." In light of this comment, explore connections between *The Duchess of Malfi* and *A Streetcar Named Desire*.

"Both plays suggest that relationships, whether romantic or familial, can only function if women submit to masculine power." To what extent is this true of *The Duchess of Malfi* and *A Streetcar Named Desire*?

How far would you agree that Webster and Williams endorse the misogynistic attitudes of their time in *The Duchess of Malfi* and *A Streetcar Named Desire*?

Both playwrights draw a lot of attention towards gender-based double standards:

- Mitch tells Blanche that she is "not clean enough" to be his wife, before attempting to rape her.

- The Cardinal declares that all women are unfaithful, whilst having an affair with Julia.

- Stanley berates Blanche and Stella for behaving "like a pair of queens" before declaring that he is "the king around here".

- Bosola mocks the "old lady" for her "scurvy face physic" and claims that all women are deceitful for their "painting", before insisting that he wear a mask himself as he murders the Duchess: "Not in mine own shape…"

Despite these instances of hypocrisy, the extent to which both playwrights champion the rights of their female characters is ambiguous. It could be suggested that they are in fact condemnatory, rather than supportive, of the protagonists.

In support of the idea that the playwrights are critical of Blanche and the Duchess, we could point out that both Webster and Williams present us with female protagonists who <u>breach and disrupt social norms</u>. As Elia Kazan points out, Blanche is "destructive"; she enters Stella and Stanley's home and causes disruption to their way of life. "This", he claims, "makes Stanley right".

The Duchess' marriage to Antonio, meanwhile, may well have been considered disruptive by a contemporary, Renaissance audience, because <u>she marries beneath her</u>, and, in doing so, violates the Great Chain of Being. This concept, which was originally classical but remained popular in Webster's time, held that the universe has a hierarchical structure that has been fixed in place by God. There is a sacrilegious element, therefore, to the Duchess' choice of an unnatural husband; she is violating the divine order of the universe. Similarly, Blanche also challenges convention through her misplaced sexual desires, because she attempts to find romance in young men, and, in doing so, contravenes the social codes of the twentieth century, and indeed today, regarding relationships with children.

The fact, therefore, that Webster and Williams present us with non-conformist and disruptive women, whose actions lead directly to tragedy, perhaps supports the notion that the playwrights are reinforcing misogynistic attitudes in their work.

This view, however, seems incongruous with the representation of society in both plays. Both playwrights appear critical of social and cultural norms, rather than the women who defy them. Just take the examples of hypocrisy mentioned on page 64: why would Webster and Williams draw so much attention to these, if they approved of the patriarchal establishment? Ferdinand and the Cardinal, moreover, are clearly villainous characters, whilst the Duchess is often painted in an admirable and noble light: "You never fixed your eye on three fair medals cast in one figure, of so different temper". Webster also had the opportunity to portray the Duchess as the "foolish woman" of William Painter's "Duchess of Malfy" (see page 40), but he did not, which suggests that he is not wholly condemnatory of her.

Another Question:

To what extent would you agree with the view that "Blanche and the Duchess are 'feminist heroines'"?

In this discussion, we'll understand "feminist heroine" to mean a woman who fights for her rights against the patriarchal societies in which the plays are set.

As mentioned previously, both women break social norms, but is this enough to be considered a "feminist heroine"?

John Webster has been referred to as a "proto-feminist" – someone who believed in or championed women's rights before the feminist movement existed. One of the most famous lines in the play is the question that the Duchess poses to Ferdinand in Act III scene ii: "Why should only I of all the other princes of the world be cased up like a holy relic?" She is asking why she should not be placed on an equal footing with the other, male or female, members of the nobility. In essence, therefore, she is asking why women are granted less freedom than men. It is a radical notion for its time.

It is difficult to imagine Blanche making a statement such as this. Rather than encouraging change and looking to the future, she clings to the past. Indeed, a Marxist interpretation of the play might consider her the personification of the **bourgeois**, slave-owning "Old South", and that, in her power struggle with Stanley, she is attempting to prevent the rise of the new American urban **proletariat**.

Blanche never has the autonomy that the Duchess has. One only has to look to the titles of the plays in order to infer this. In *The Duchess of Malfi*, the Duchess is the **eponymous** figure; the play is her story. By contrast, Williams names his play after the streetcar which carries Blanche to Elysian Fields - "where I'm not wanted and where I'm ashamed to be." As we discussed on page 30, the Streetcar – as indicated by its name, "desire" – is a metaphor for sexual passion. Both Stella and Blanche recognise the symbolism of the streetcar, and they discuss it in scene IV, in which Blanche urges Stella to leave her abusive husband and is appalled by the overwhelming extent of her passion for him:

Blanche: What you are talking about is brutal desire – just – Desire! The name of that rattle-trap street-car that bangs through the Quarter, up one old narrow lane and down another...

Stella: Haven't you ever ridden on that street-car?

Blanche: It brought me here.

Scene IV

It is Blanche's promiscuous history which has ruined her, and which in turn has driven her, like the streetcar, to Stella and Stanley's home. Thus, whilst the Duchess is clearly the heroine of her story, *A Streetcar Named Desire* is named after a symbol for Blanche's powerlessness; she is a passenger, being driven by forces which seem beyond her control. It is important to remember key differences such as this, as well as similarities, when you compare the two protagonists.

> "...the kind of travel particularised by a streetcar fits well with the play's representation of desire as a driving force taking characters to destinations which are, at best, very approximate choices."
>
> Jackie Shead, "*A Streetcar Named Desire*: Life Luggage", *The English Review*

One of the interesting features of *The Duchess of Malfi* is that, in contrast to his independent-minded, self-governing wife, Antonio appears a markedly unheroic figure. This is particularly the case in Act II Scene ii, in which Ferdinand enters his sister's bedchamber and orders her to kill herself. Antonio only returns to the stage once Ferdinand has vacated it, which gives the audience the impression that he was hiding and waiting until he could be sure that the villain was gone.

The proposal scene is a famous example of the Duchess' independence. It is she who proposes to Antonio, and she who puts the ring on his finger. To borrow Brian Gibbons' words, the Duchess "demands Antonio attend the presence, teases him, woos and wins him, thereby excitingly reversing the gender-roles." Even after her death, the Duchess remains the centre of the story; she is the reason for everything that follows. As Jaqueline Pearson points out, "the heroine dies well before the end of the play so that the significance of her death can be explored".

Blanche lacks this independence. She breaks convention through her sexuality, but – unlike the Duchess, who marries Antonio because she wants to do so - Blanche's actions appear beyond her control:

"After the death of Allan – intimacies with strangers was all I seemed to fill my empty heart with... I think it was panic, just panic, that drove me from one to another, hunting for some protection, here and there, in the most – unlikely places".

Scene IX

As she confesses in this passage, Blanche looks to men for protection. This is observable elsewhere in the play: she describes Mitch as a "cleft in the rock of the world that I could hide in", and looks to an old admirer, Shep Huntleigh, for help after the "Poker Night" scene, in which Stanley beats his pregnant wife. Both of these men (and it is left ambiguous as to whether the latter even exists) fail Blanche in the end.

Blanche's mistake, therefore, lies in her reliance on men. As Simon Bubb explains, "*A Streetcar Named Desire* dramatises a world marked by great pain and darkness. The tragedy that unfolds is one in which men are ultimately shown not as active agents of redemption from this suffering, but as its cause." By looking to men to solve her problems, rather than herself, Blanche does not relieve herself of her suffering, but deepens it.

Other Women:

It is certainly possible to be asked a question which focusses on Blanche and the Duchess. However, remember that questions concerning "women" in general are <u>not only referring to these two characters</u> but also to the other women in the plays. Always try and look beyond the obvious, if you can.

Both Julia and Stella could be regarded as passive women who submit to their manipulative sexual partners:

- After the pregnant Stella receives a "blow" during the "Poker Night" scene, she retreats from Stanley into Eunice's apartment, but returns to him when he cries out to her: "I want my baby down here".

- In Act II scene iv, Julia responds to the Cardinal's insults by declaring that she will "go home to my husband". Nevertheless, however, she obeys him when he orders her to stay.

Stella and Julia, therefore, are alike in that they both place themselves at the mercy of their respective sexual partners.

It is possible to interpret Stella and Julia in a very negative light. It could be suggested, for example, that they are only concerned with their own selfish and base sexual instincts. These take precedence over everything in their lives, including their sense of what is right: Julia has an adulterous affair with an evidently corrupt and villainous man, whilst Stella has her sister committed to an institution for the mentally ill in order to preserve her life with

Stanley: "I couldn't believe her story and go on living with Stanley".

> "Stella ignores the needs of others and eventually adopts her own illusion. Life with Stanley – sex with Stanley – is her highest value. Her refusal to accept Blanche's story of the rape is a commitment to self-preservation rather than love, and thus Stella contributes to Blanche's disintegration".
>
> J. M. McGlinn

Directors of *The Duchess of Malfi* often present Julia as a licentious figure, wearing a suggestive costume. It is possible to support this interpretation with evidence from the text: after all, she is willing to have an affair with the Cardinal, and her feelings for Bosola arise with comical speed. Indeed, some critics argue that Webster intended Julia to act as a **foil** to the Duchess; she is meant to appear base and wanton, in order to make the Duchess' sexuality appear, by contrast, admirable and romantic.

Ultimately, it is Julia's promiscuity which leads to her death, since it is her lover who murders her, by ordering her to kiss the poisoned Bible. The nature of her death further underscores this point: Julia dies in the act of kissing.

Of course, it is also possible to view Julia and Stella in a more sympathetic light. It could be pointed out, for example, that they are both women attempting to live in viciously patriarchal societies. Though we may not condone their actions, as human beings we can sympathise with their instinct to survive.

Frank Whigham follows this line of argument in his analysis of *The Duchess of Malfi*, in which he suggests that Julia is not obsessed with sex; rather, she uses sex to search for protection in an unkind world: Julia is "drawn to power, to men who can [....] make their women significant or safe."

Moreover, it is important to remember that, in spite of their flaws, these women are also victims. Julia is murdered, whilst Stella is beaten and abused.

"Stella is a refined girl who has found a kind of salvation or realization, *but at a terrific price*. She keeps her eyes closed, even stays in bed as much as possible so that she won't realise, won't *feel* the pain of this terrific price."

Elia Kazan,
director of the 1951 film of *A Streetcar Named Desire*

Williams ends his play with a striking, and ambiguous, final image:

> *She sobs with inhuman abandon. There is something luxurious in her complete surrender to crying now her sister is gone.*
>
> **Stanley:** [*voluptuously, soothingly*]: Now, honey. Now, love. Now, now love. [*He kneels beside her and his fingers find the opening of her blouse.*] Now, now, love. Now, love…

It has been suggested that Stanley is noticeably weaker in this scene. Before, Stella had been besotted with her husband; now he is desperately attempting to grasp her attention. Carla J. McDonough endorses this view, suggesting that Stanley grasps at Stella "like a child clings to a mother after waking from a bad dream". Conversely, it could be suggested that this image reinforces Stanley's victory over Blanche. Throughout the play, the antagonist and protagonist had fought over possession of Stella (both repeatedly refer to her as "baby"), and perhaps this image serves to reinforce his control over her.

The use of language here, moreover, is also ambiguous. Does the repetition of "Now, love" really suggest that Stanley is attempting to comfort Stella? Or could the word "Now" be interpreted as a command (he is telling her to have sex with him "now")? He has, after all, been waiting for Blanche to leave in order to have "them coloured lights going" again; is he taking the first opportunity - the moment Blanche has been institutionalised - to do so? This interpretation, which presents Stanley in a particularly sinister light, could be supported by the fact that "his fingers find the opening of her blouse".

Akin to Julia and Stella, Eunice also submits to her sexual partner, Steve: in Scene V, the audience see the couple sharing a "tight embrace" a few moments after he has assaulted her. As Susan Koprince argues, "Eunice and Steve are the facsimile of a dysfunctional family which normalises Stanley's abuse." Eunice and Steve's unhealthy relationship informs Stanley that domestic violence of this kind will go unpunished.

Men and Masculinity:

When you are asked a question explicitly concerning women or femininity, it is important that you do not digress by discussing men and masculinity. <u>Remain focussed on the question</u>.

However, you may get a broader question concerning gender, or the tensions between the sexes. In which case, a discussion of masculinity is certainly relevant.

<u>Of course, you could get a question on masculinity in its own right:</u>

How far would you agree that masculinity is a destructive force in *The Duchess of Malfi* and *A Streetcar Named Desire*?

"The men in both plays are uniformly cruel." To what extent is this true of *The Duchess of Malfi* and *A Streetcar Named Desire*?

> "Tensions arise because the men of both plays are frightened by female independence and seek to control women, by whatever means necessary." To what extent can this comment be applied to *The Duchess of Malfi* and *A Streetcar Named Desire*?

We discussed Antonio's unheroic character earlier, and how this serves to emphasise the Duchess' independence and strength of character. Could his weakness serve to parallel that of Mitch in *A Streetcar Named Desire*? Initially, Mitch appears to be the hero who will save Blanche from misery and destitution (Scene VI is arguably the most hopeful of the whole play), but he actually serves to deepen her misery by bitterly, and hypocritically, rejecting her.

> Something to consider:
>
> How do Webster and Williams characterise the men of their plays? Are there any characteristics which are shared by them all?

It is certainly fair to suggest that the men of the plays enjoy greater freedom than the female characters:

Duchess: Were I a man I'd beat that counterfeit face into thy other

Act III scene v

Stella: There's not a word of truth in it and if I were a man and this creature had dared to invent such things in my presence –

Scene VII

Both Stella and the Duchess accept that men are at liberty to behave in certain ways, whilst women are not. In the above cases, it is physical violence that is being deemed appropriate for a man but inappropriate for a woman.

Are the men of the plays characterised by a propensity for physical violence?

Williams' stage directions suggest that Stanley is a powerful and violent character: he "hurls", "slams", "shoves", "rips" and "lurches". He responds aggressively to being given orders, especially by women. We see this in Scene II, when he snaps at Stella for telling him to come outside whilst Blanche dresses ("Since when do you give me orders?") and again in Scene III, when he attacks her. In scene VIII, he begins smashing plates after Stella tells him to "go wash up and help me clear the table". Aggression, therefore, is a key characteristic of Stanley's masculinity.

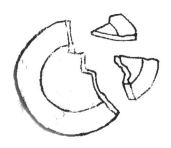

"What do you think you are? A pair of queens? Remember what Huey Long said – 'Every Man is a King!' And I am the king around here, so don't forget it!"

A Streetcar Named Desire, Scene VIII

Ferdinand and the Cardinal are similarly willing to act violently towards others, but they differ from Stanley in that they prefer not to dirty their own hands. At the beginning of the play, we learn that Bosola "fell into the galleys" for committing a crime (which Delio believes to be murder) on behalf of the

Cardinal, for which he is not rewarded: "I have done you better service than to be slighted thus." Later, of course, he is instructed by Ferdinand to carry out the torture and murder of the Duchess.

This is the result of differences in class and status: the Aragonian brothers are wealthy aristocrats; they wield the power and wealth that is required to use (and exploit) men like Bosola, who are desperate to climb the social ladder. Stanley, meanwhile, is a working-class man.

Nevertheless, the three men are perhaps more alike than different. Both Ferdinand and Stanley, for example, have invasive relationships with the female protagonists: Ferdinand acquires a key to his sister's bedchamber, and sneaks in at night to give her the poniard, whilst Stanley shamelessly roots through Blanche's belongings. In addition, the two men even try to invade the minds of these women: Ferdinand tells Bosola that his sister "needs be mad" and sends "madfolk" into her room in an attempt to destroy her sanity, whilst Stanley is often tormenting Blanche psychologically (such as when he gives her the bus ticket to Laurel on her birthday). *These psychological power games are discussed at greater length on page 120.*

Similarly, Ferdinand and Stanley are also alike in that they are deeply emotional characters, driven by rage to commit rash acts of violence and cruelty.

Consider the following examples, and see if you can come up with any more:

Ferdinand	Stanley
"Would I could be the one That I might toss her palace 'bout her ears Root up her goodly forests, blast her meads And lay her general territory to waste As she hath done her honours." Act II scene v	*"Stanley stalks fiercely through the portières into the bedroom. He crosses to the small white radio and snatches it off the table. With a shouted oath, he tosses the instrument out of the window."* Scene III
"Damn her, that body of hers, While that my blood ran pure in't, was more worth Than that which thou wouldst comfort, called a soul." Act IV scene ii	*"He advances and disappears. There is the sound of a blow. Stella cries out … something is overturned with a crash."* Scene III

"I would have their bodies Burnt in a coal pit with the ventage stopped, That their curse smoke might not ascend to heaven; Or dip the sheets they lie in, in pitch or sulphur, Wrap them in't and then light them like a match..." Act II scene v	"Hey, canary bird! Toots! Get *OUT* of the *BATHROOM*! [...] *The bathroom door flies open and Blanche emerges... as Stanley crosses past her, a frightened look appears in her face, almost a look of panic. He doesn't look at her but slams the bathroom door shut as he goes in.*" Scene VII
"I will stamp him into a cullis, flay off his skin... Hence! Hence! You are all of you like beasts for sacrifice! There's nothing left of you but tongue and belly, flattery and lechery!" Act V scene ii	"*He hurls a plate to the floor.* **STANLEY:** That's how I'll clear the table! [*He seizes her arm.*] Don't ever talk that way to me!" Scene VIII

By contrast, the Cardinal is not characterised by this wild rage and violent anger. Indeed, it is his apparent lack of emotion that makes him sinister; he is cold, calculating and unmoved by the damage he causes to the lives of others. Whilst his brother is driven to madness by guilt and grief after the murder of the Duchess, the Cardinal is plotting how best to conceal the crime: "I must feign somewhat..." Perhaps he is at his most sinister, however, in Act V scene ii, in which he murders Julia, his former mistress.

In this scene, Julia dies after being instructed by the Cardinal to kiss a poisoned Bible (see page 34). It is important to remember that this is a carefully calculated and planned murder; the Cardinal does not lash out and strike Julia, as we might expect of Ferdinand. Rather, he has the poisoned book in his pocket during the conversation that precedes her death. During this conversation, the Cardinal teases Julia, pretending that he is unwilling to reveal his secret (that he ordered his sister's murder) to her: "Satisfy thy longing, the only way to make thee keep my counsel is not to tell thee." Finally, he alludes to poison - his method of murder - by telling her that she will be unable to keep such a terrible secret:

"'tis a secret that like a ling'ring poison may chance lie spread in thy veins, and kill thee seven year hence."

Act V scene ii

The Cardinal alludes to poison here - which will indeed soon kill Julia – in order to amuse himself, which further emphasises his callous character. The long adjective "ling'ring", moreover, perhaps provides a sense of relish.

"In this lethal but trivial world the Cardinal plays a chief role. His cool, unemotional detachment is more terrifying than Ferdinand's impassioned raving."

Lee Bliss, *The World's Perspective: John Webster and the Jacobean Drama*

In Ferdinand and the Cardinal, Webster provides two very different, but equally destructive, images of masculinity: the former is explosive, violent and agitated ("a most perverse and turbulent nature"), whilst the other is aloof, cold and unfeeling.

We have already discussed some of the similarities between Stanley and Ferdinand; like Ferdinand, Stanley has a propensity for stormy outbursts. Nevertheless, it is also possible to draw some parallels between Stanley and the other Aragonian brother. Like the Cardinal, Stanley has the potential to be callous and cunning. Consider the following examples:

- In Scene IV, Stanley overhears Blanche talking to Stella; she calls him "ape-like", "an animal", a "survivor from the stone age", and a "brute". Stanley does not burst in on the conversation in a fit of rage; rather, he waits patiently outside and listens to everything, "licking his lips" like a predator. Finally, when he does enter the room, he embraces his wife and "grins through the curtains at Blanche".

- Stanley plans to destroy Blanche by collecting information about her behind her back: "I found out some things! [...] Things I already suspected. But now I got proof from the most reliable sources – which I have checked on!"

- In Scene VIII, Stanley gives Blanche "a little birthday remembrance": a bus ticket to Laurel. Though "she tries to laugh", this 'gift' is too distressing to ignore, and Blanche is forced to rush to the bathroom to vomit. This attack is premeditated: Stanley bought the ticket in advance of Blanche's birthday dinner, and planned to give it to her. In addition, he is completely unmoved by her distress, and prepares to go bowling: he "changes into a brilliant silk bowling shirt".

Clearly, the plays' antagonists do not offer positive examples of masculinity, but, as we discussed on page 78 (and will discuss a little more on page 94) it is difficult to suggest that Mitch or Antonio offer much brighter alternatives. The former attempts to rape Blanche, whilst the latter hides whilst his wife is being threatened with a dagger.

In his analysis of *A Streetcar Named Desire*, Simon Bubb suggests that there are no positive representations of masculinity in the play. Read the extract on the next page and see if you agree with his argument. In the space below the text box, write quotations from the plays which support and challenge his point-of-view. This will help you to *assess* critical opinions, rather than simply embedding them into your work.

"This is a play in which there is not a single male character to whom we can look for a truly positive embodiment of masculinity [...] There is one knight in shining armour, of course. He is the respectful 'gentleman' and millionaire, Shep Huntleigh. However, he too fails to come to Blanche's rescue. Typically, the one figure who might provide a lasting hope turns out to have been a fantasy all along."

Simon Bubb, "Presentations of Masculinity – A Streetcar Named Desire", English & Media Centre

Class and Power

Both *The Duchess of Malfi* and *A Streetcar Named Desire* involve struggles for power. In each, the audience witness characters attempting to control or manipulate other characters. Power is security in the worlds of these plays, and, when characters sense that they are losing it, they often respond rashly, or with aggression.

Some questions to consider...

"The upper classes are shamelessly vilified; it is impossible to sympathise with them." In light of this comment, explore connections between *The Duchess of Malfi* and *A Streetcar Named Desire*.

How far would you agree with the idea that, in *The Duchess of Malfi* and *A Streetcar Named Desire*, Webster and Williams "show us that human society is no different from the jungle"?

> "By the end of the plays, the established social order has clearly been weakened." To what extent can this comment be applied to *The Duchess of Malfi* and *A Streetcar Named Desire*?

> "All of the characters are only concerned with increasing and protecting their own personal power." In light of this comment, explore connections between *The Duchess of Malfi* and *A Streetcar Named Desire*.

Blanche and the Duchess are clearly at the centre of these plays, but it is also interesting to observe the power relationships between men. Stanley, Ferdinand and the Cardinal, for example, all derive their power from the circle of servile men they surround themselves with. These men do little or nothing to prevent the cruelty and violence of the antagonists. In the case of *The Duchess of Malfi*, these are the sycophantic courtiers; figures such as Roderigo and Grisolan. As the following grotesque simile, delivered by Bosola, suggests, these sycophants serve to damage and corrupt the court:

"He and his brother are like plum trees that grow crooked over standing pools: they are rich, and o'erladen with fruit, but none but crows, pies and caterpillars feed on them. Could I be one of their flatt'ring panders, I would hang on their ears till I were full, and then drop off."

Act I scene i

This passage launches the motif of pests and disease that will persist throughout the play (see page 29). It also deliberately parodies Antonio's description of the French court, at the very beginning of the play, which is unpolluted by "flatt'ring sycophants" and "infamous persons". As Theodora A. Jankowski notes, "Antonio's description of the ideal French court...acts as a touchstone for the accepted Renaissance ideal of court life..." By placing this description right at the beginning of the play, Webster establishes a benchmark for measuring an honest and honourable court, which draws attention to the corruption of the Italian court throughout the play. These "flatt'ring panders", moreover, were perhaps intended to criticise the favouritism and vice which existed in the court of James I (see page 37)

"When I'm losing you want to eat! Ante up! Openers? Openers! Get off the table, Mitch. Nothing belongs on a poker table but cards, chips and whiskey."

A Streetcar Named Desire, Scene III

Though not of a high social status in the same way as Ferdinand and the Cardinal, Stanley wields a similar kind of power over Pablo, Steve and Mitch. This is made particularly apparent in "The Poker Night" scene. Consider Williams' use of dialogue here: exclamatory commands and **imperative verbs** are used to illustrate the fact that Stanley is in command ("Ante up!", "Shut up", "go home"). His obsession with asserting his power is repeatedly reinforced. Have a look at the phone call that he makes in scene VIII, for example: "I'm the team captain, aren't I?". The audience are given the impression that Stanley is not only struggling for power over Blanche; rather, he has this struggle with everyone in his life.

In Scene IV, Blanche uses prehistoric images and animalistic metaphors to describe the previous evening:

"Night falls and the other apes gather! There in the front of the cave, all grunting like him, and swilling and gnawing and hulking!"

Scene IV

This comment, which clearly reflects the influence of evolutionary biology and **Social Darwinism** (a strand of thought which is often associated with modern playwrights, such as Ibsen and Beckett), serves to depict Stanley as an 'alpha male' amongst his loyal and subservient pack.

By describing the other men as "grunting like him", moreover, Williams seems to imply that the other men are actively attempting to emulate Stanley. This marks a striking parallel to the courtiers in *The Duchess of Malfi*, who Ferdinand directly orders to follow his example: "take fire when I give fire… laugh when I laugh". This command suggests that Ferdinand actively desires their sycophantic flattery; he, like Stanley (who destroys Blanche partly as an attempt to deflect Mitch's devotion away from her and back to him) is left insecure and unstable without his supporters.

In both *The Duchess of Malfi* and *A Streetcar Named Desire,* minor characters watch on as the more powerful **antagonists** behave with violence and cruelty. Are we, as an audience, meant to condemn their passivity? Should be hold them responsible for the plays' tragic conclusions?

Perhaps it would be interesting to focus on specific characters here: let's consider Bosola and Mitch.

Both of these characters are associated with the main antagonists, but they are also carefully distinguished from them. In both cases, we are given the impression, through the remarks of other characters, that Bosola and Mitch are essentially good-natured:

Antonio: ...I have heard he's very valiant. This foul melancholy will poison all his goodness.

Act I scene i

Blanche: That one seems – superior to the others. [...] I thought he had a sort of sensitive look.

Scene III

Bosola and Mitch have had their perspectives of the world shaped by the societies in which they live. Bosola, for example, believes that he can only survive if he serves as the "creature" of the "Aragonian brethren". It is this belief which "poison[s] all his goodness"; as he remarks later, he "sought to appear a true servant", rather than an "honest man". This leads him to committing acts of great evil, such as the murder of the Duchess. Similarly, Mitch – despite his "sort of sensitive look" – ultimately accepts the cruel gender-based double standards of his time, which lead him to rejecting (and ruining) Blanche: he bitterly, and hypocritically, declares that she is "not clean enough" to be his wife. Both characters, therefore, are products of their time.

As we have just mentioned, Bosola views the world in terms of a strict, social hierarchy, in which he accepts - without question - that he must serve his betters, regardless of their moral character. As a result, he is overcome with a kind of joyous confusion when he hears that the Duchess has refused to obey the rules of this rigid hierarchy, by marrying Antonio purely on the basis of his merit:

"Do I not dream? Can this ambitious age have so much goodness in't as to prefer a man merely for worth...? Possible?"

Act III scene ii

Look at how the multiple rhetorical questions here are used to emphasise his incredulous amazement.

Though Bosola informs Ferdinand that Antonio is the Duchess' husband, this moment could be seen to mark the beginning of a transformation in the **malcontent**'s character. After this, Bosola will attempt, albeit unsuccessfully, to remedy his mistakes by murdering the Cardinal and, in doing so, saving Antonio.

The audience witness something of the reverse in Mitch. As Simon Bubb identifies, instead of offering a "positive alternative to Stanley's insensitive, bullish masculinity", Mitch "end[s] up imitating it". This idea

96

is reinforced by the way in which Williams structures his play: in Scene IX, he has Mitch destroy the paper lantern and attempt to rape Blanche, both of which will be repeated by Stanley in Scene X. Thus, the audience are left with the impression that Mitch, far from being a "cleft in the rock of the world" for Blanche to hide in, is simply a weak portrait of her main abuser.

Of course, neither character is able to free themselves, truly, from their position within the social order. By inadvertently murdering Antonio, Bosola carries out the Cardinal's wishes, and thus he remains, to the end, "a true servant" to the "Aragonian brethren", rather than an "honest man". Similarly, the final image that the audience have of Mitch is of him "sobbing" as he "collapse[s]" on the poker table in Scene XI, at the mercy of Stanley's abuse: "hold this bone-headed cry-baby!" This, therefore, serves to parallel Scene III, in which Mitch, whilst also at the poker table, is similarly ridiculed by Stanley: "hurry back and we'll fix you a sugar-tit". In structuring their plays in this way, both playwrights seem to suggest that there was never much hope of change or development for Bosola and Mitch. Rather, they are both held rigidly in their social roles. What does this suggest about the structure of society and the possession of power within the plays?

The extent to which these characters bear responsibility for the plays' tragedies is a matter of debate. Though it seems unfair to suggest that they are equally as culpable as the main antagonists, it also seems too generous to acquit them of blame entirely.

Secrecy and Deceit

An interesting feature of both plays is that, in each, the protagonists are deceivers. In both cases, these secrets are related to sex. The Duchess has taken a second husband from beneath her own rank, which she must conceal because it violates the promise she has made to her two brothers. Blanche's promiscuous history, meanwhile, must be concealed if she is to achieve financial security for herself through a second marriage.

Consider the following questions...

How far do you agree with the view that, in *The Duchess of Malfi* and *A Streetcar Named Desire*, "the audience are presented with societies in which secrecy and deceit are rife"?

How far would you agree that Webster and Williams investigate the relationship between truth and illusion in *The Duchess of Malfi* and *A Streetcar Named Desire?*

> "Though we cannot sympathise with them, the antagonists have more integrity than the protagonists." To what extent is this true of *The Duchess of Malfi* and *A Streetcar Named Desire*?

Let's begin by considering how Blanche and the Duchess deceive others, and draw connections between the two texts:

Blanche first enters the stage wearing "a white suit with a fluffy bodice". Traditionally, the colour white is used to symbolise virginity. By wearing this colour, therefore, is Blanche attempting, insincerely, to present herself as a virgin to the other characters?

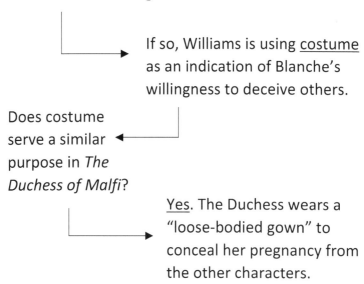

If so, Williams is using <u>costume</u> as an indication of Blanche's willingness to deceive others.

Does costume serve a similar purpose in *The Duchess of Malfi*?

<u>Yes</u>. The Duchess wears a "loose-bodied gown" to conceal her pregnancy from the other characters.

This is a good example of how you should be thinking when you approach the two plays during your revision. If you make a point about one play, consider if it applies to the other play too. Thinking in this way will ensure that you are capable of making the precise, purposeful links that are required for a high AO4 mark.

Williams and Webster also <u>structure</u> their plays in order to expose the fact that the protagonists are attempting to deceive:

- In the opening scene of *The Duchess of Malfi*, the Duchess promises her brothers that she will "never marry", after which Webster has the brothers exit the stage. This enables him to have the Duchess inform the audience, in **soliloquy**, that she intends to "assay" the "dangerous venture" of disobeying them –showing us that she is very much capable of deceiving others.

- In the opening scene of *A Streetcar Named Desire*, Williams instructs the actress playing Blanche to pour herself "a half tumbler of whiskey" from Stanley's cabinet, before carefully "replac[ing] the bottle and wash[ing] out the tumbler at the sink" (an act which itself illustrates her skill at concealing information about herself). By then having Stella enter the stage and offer her sister a "shot" – to which Blanche replies that she "rarely touch[es] it" - the audience is alerted to Blanche's capacity for deceit.

Something to consider:

Looking at the texts, what do you think playwrights' opinions of secrecy and deceit are?

Both Blanche and the Duchess suffer as a result of their attempts to deceive others. Do you think Webster and Williams intended their plays to serve a **didactic** purpose, and that the suffering of the protagonists is a form of punishment, warning the audience to be aware of the perils of lying?

Or do their plays suggest that it is not always morally wrong to tell lies?

Look at the questions in the box above. Let's begin by trying to support the idea that deceit is not always inherently wrong in the two plays:

- According to Michael Billington, Blanche tells lies "as a protection against solitude and desperation". She sees them not as mischievous or morally wrong, but as "magic" – something miraculous which helps her to cope.

- It is only through secrecy and deceit that the Duchess and Antonio are able to preserve their happy marriage: "I prithee when were we so merry?"

- The Duchess' decision to pretend that Antonio has wronged her – which accounts for Ferdinand's leaving "in a whirlwind" and allows Antonio to flee to Ancona – is described as a "noble lie". This **oxymoronic** phrase suggests that deceit can be put to honourable purposes, such as the saving of a life.

- Bosola deceives the Duchess as she dies by telling her that Antonio is "reconciled to [her] brothers". This provides her with peace, as indicated by her final word: "Mercy."

Thus, though it is true that secrecy and deceit are rife in these plays, it is questionable whether they are always regarded as inherently immoral and wrong.

Of course, it is possible to challenge this idea by pointing out that the Duchess loses everything as a result of her decision to deceive her brothers, whilst Blanche's lies and illusions never truly make her happy. Indeed, as Felicia Hardison Londré points out, it is only when Blanche is being honest with Mitch in Scene VI that she gains "what she has not been able to achieve in two months or so of artful deceit: a proposal of marriage."

Another Question:

Is it those who strive to uncover secrets, rather than those who keep them, who are presented in a negative light?

The antagonists in both plays are made deeply insecure and anxious by the possibility of secrets escaping their attention, and thus – in both cases – they endeavour to uncover and expose them.

We discussed the significance of the paper lantern on page 32, and how, when Mitch tears it down in Scene IX, this serves to symbolise the destruction of Blanche's façade.

Blanche's trunk serves a similar symbolic purpose. This is because it could be seen to represent her past; it is her "life luggage", to borrow Jackie

Shead's phrase. Thus, Stanley's frustrated search through it in Scene II perhaps represents his desire to uncover the secrets of her past in order to destroy her.

"Pearls! Ropes of them! What is this sister of yours, a deep-sea diver who brings up sunken treasures? [...] Bracelets of solid gold, too! Where are your pearls and gold bracelets?"

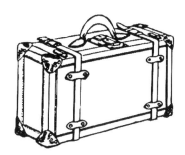

A Streetcar Named Desire,
Scene II

"Travellers have luggage, and experience also brings psychological and emotional baggage. Both are evident in the content and arrangement of Blanche's trunk, who importance is made clear by her comment, 'Everything I own is in that trunk'. [...] Stanley's intrusion into the trunk marks the beginning of an invasion of Blanche's self, which does not cease until his ultimate penetration – rape."

Jackie Shead, "*A Streetcar Named Desire*:
Life Luggage", *The English Review*

It is significant, moreover, that – at the beginning of Scene X – Blanche's trunk "hangs open with flowery dresses thrown across it." This indicates that, by this point, Blanche's promiscuous past has been fully exposed. Her "life luggage", in other words, is now on display.

The "Aragonian brethren" are similarly intent on exposing the Duchess' secrets. In order to do this, however, they use secretive methods themselves, rather than Stanley's method of stubborn force. They employ Bosola to spy on the Duchess, for example, under the pretence that he will serve as the manager of her horses. Later, Ferdinand pretends that he intends for his sister to marry the Count Malateste, in an attempt to probe the truth about Antonio.

Indeed, the play concludes with Delio remarking on the value of honesty:

"Integrity of life is fame's best friend,

which nobly, beyond death, shall crown the end."

Act V scene v

This is a quality that all of the major characters lacked in *The Duchess of Malfi*. In *Streetcar*, meanwhile, even those who possess it are far from being virtuous.

Death and Mortality

Both *The Duchess of Malfi* and *A Streetcar Named Desire* are haunted by ominous symbols, which serve to herald tragedy. The sheer number of deaths in Webster's play seems to suggest that human life is perilous and fragile. Williams, meanwhile, focusses on the fear of death rather than dying itself, and how this fear can torment the sanity of human beings.

<u>Some questions to consider...</u>

"None of the characters are truly powerful; they are all at the mercy of time and death." To what extent is this true of *The Duchess of Malfi* and *A Streetcar Named Desire*?

"Death, or the fear of it, has the greatest influence on the actions of the characters, even more so than sexual desire." In light of this comment, explore connections between *The Duchess of Malfi* and *A Streetcar Named Desire*.

In *A Streetcar Named Desire*, Blanche's fear of death is expressed from the outset. In the very first scene, she tells Stella (in distressed, fractured speech) that she was forced to witness the "long parade to the graveyard" at Belle Reve as her relatives died one by one: "Why, the Grim Reaper had put up his tent on our doorstop!"

Williams himself suffered from an acute fear of death, which was the product of a near-fatal childhood illness. This manifested itself in extreme hypochondria; in 1946, for example, he became convinced that he was dying of pancreatic cancer. Blanche's fear of death, as well as the ominous symbols which persist throughout the play, are perhaps a reflection of Williams' own anxiety.

As we mentioned in the discussion of "ominous imagery" on page 35, both playwrights make use of menacing symbols and motifs in order to emphasise the omnipresent threat of death in their plays, and establish an atmosphere of foreboding.

One such symbol in *The Duchess of Malfi* is Antonio's handkerchief; his embroidered initials are "drowned in blood" as a result of a nose bleed, which serves to foreshadow his death. Similarly, the "blind Mexican woman in a dark shawl" selling flowers "that lower class Mexicans display at funerals" in *A Streetcar Named Desire* could be considered a representation of death.

The woman's "barely audible" call of "flores para los muertos" ("flowers for the dead") deeply affects Blanche. It triggers the memory of Allan's suicide – as indicated by the "fad[ing] in" of the Varsouviana polka. Thus, whilst Antonio dismisses his ominous sign, unwisely, as "mere accident", Blanche remains sensitive to, and fearful of, reminders of death. This terror is indicated by the fact that her dialogue becomes fractured and fearful after the Mexican woman has entered the stage:

"What? Oh! Somebody outside... I – I lived in a house where dying old women remembered their dead men..."

Scene X

It is interesting, therefore, that the tragedy of *A Streetcar Named Desire* does not end with death – despite Blanche's fear of it – whilst all of the major characters in *The Duchess of Malfi* – who are frequently dismissive of foreboding symbols (consider not only Antonio's reaction to the handkerchief mentioned above, but also the Duchess in Act III scene ii: "Thou art a superstitious fool") – do suffer this fate. Perhaps in both cases this serves to underscore the idea that, whether pessimistic or optimistic, none of the characters are able to predict their fates.

Death and Desire:

In Scene IX of *A Streetcar Named Desire*, Blanche tells Mitch that "the opposite [of death] is desire". This puts into words an idea which Williams has established from the outset; in the opening scene, Blanche tells Eunice that

"They told me to take a streetcar named Desire, and then transfer to one called Cemeteries and ride six blocks and get off at – Elysian Fields!"

Elysian Fields is the street that Stella and Stanley live on. It is also a classical **allusion** to a part of the Underworld which, according to Greek mythology, was occupied by heroes after their deaths.

We discussed the symbolism surrounding the streetcar named Desire on page 30. With this discussion in mind, have a look at Blanche's journey, which takes place immediately prior to the events of the play:

A streetcar named Desire

A streetcar named Cemeteries

Elysian Fields

Metaphorically, Blanche's promiscuous history has killed her, and thus the play takes place in a kind of afterlife, in which she will be punished, cruelly, for her past sexual activity. Through this, Williams shows us that death and desire are not only opposites; rather, they are linked – the former will always lead to the latter.

Desire could also be seen to lead to death in *The Duchess of Malfi*. It is the Duchess and Antonio's sexual relationship that will set the bloody events of the play in motion. Antonio seems to recognise this: he claims that there "is a saucy an ambitious devil... dancing" in the circle of his wedding ring. Moreover - as we will discuss further in the "Family Relationships" section – it is Ferdinand's implied incestuous feelings for his sister that lead him to tormenting and murdering her.

Brian Gibbons lends weight to this idea by suggesting that the torture of the Duchess is intended to be "an inverted wedding celebration". He argues that – far from being a chaotic scene of horror and disorder – the torture of the Duchess is a "sequence" with a "design". Take a look at some of the details he picks out and the parallels he draws:

> "The Madmen constitute an anti-masque and charivari... As Bellman, Bosola gives her macabre presents from her brothers, a coffin, cord and bell. The dirge is the exact inversion of an epithalamion or wedding-song; then comes the pronouncement of the death sentence, strangling; finally, according to this pattern, the noose is a wedding ring of death".
>
> From the introduction to the Methuen Drama edition of *The Duchess of Malfi*, pg XV

If we accept Gibbons' interpretation, it seems that Webster is trying to emphasise the connection between desire and death. Akin to Williams' streetcars, Desire and Cemeteries, the spectacle surrounding the torture and murder of the Duchess adds emphasis to the fact that her marriage to Antonio has led directly to her death.

Something to consider:

In both *The Duchess of Malfi* and *A Streetcar Named Desire*, the audience are shown the painful and powerful effects of grief.

Both Blanche and Ferdinand mourn the death of a loved one, and both are driven to madness by this grief. Their suffering is compounded, furthermore, by the fact that they both bear responsibility and guilt for this death.

A useful task would be to draw a grid, with "Ferdinand" written at the top of one column and "Blanche" in the other, which compares and contrasts the presentation of grief, death and madness in these two cases. Include direct quotes from the plays, as well as relevant context and critical views.

This is also a helpful preliminary task before we begin the following section on "Madness".

Madness

Madness is perhaps the inevitable product of the cruel and comfortless societies in which the plays are set. In the case of *A Streetcar Named Desire*, Blanche's mental decline serves to reveal how wholly she has been destroyed by her abusers, who have invaded her mind as well as her body. Ferdinand's madness, meanwhile, is caused by the guilt he experiences after having participated in the cruelty which permeates his corrupt world: "My sister! Oh my sister, there's the cause on't!" Both playwrights, therefore, seem to suggest that, when cruelty and violence are commonplace and inescapable, madness will inevitably manifest itself in some form.

Consider the following questions...

To what extent do you agree with the view that, "madness is the product of repressed sexual desire" in *The Duchess of Malfi* and *A Streetcar Named Desire*?

How far do you agree with the view that,
"Webster presents madness as a hyperbolic,
almost comic, spectacle, whilst Williams
considers it a deeply tragic and complex
phenomenon"?

"Society itself is shown to be mad, rather than
specific individuals." In light of this statement,
explore connections between *The Duchess of
Malfi* and *A Streetcar Named Desire*.

To what extent do you agree with the view that,
"madness is presented as a form of punishment
for wrongdoing" in *The Duchess of Malfi* and *A
Streetcar Named Desire*?

As we discussed briefly in the "Death and Mortality"
section, both Blanche and Ferdinand are responsible
for the deaths of loved ones, and the guilt they
experience as a result of this leads them to madness.
Their torment is seemingly perpetual; it involves
desperate self-loathing and a detachment from

reality. This depiction of guilt and madness could lead us to posing the following question...

Something to consider:

Do you think that madness is presented as a fate worse than death in these plays?

Though Blanche's fear of death is expressed from the outset (see page 109), her tragic fate is not to die but to lose her mind. In *The Duchess of Malfi*, meanwhile, Ferdinand is intent on making his sister lose possession of her mind – "she'll needs be mad" – and arranges an "antimasque" (subverting the court masque, a form of entertainment in the Renaissance), in which the "madfolk" from the "common hospital" enter her bedroom and sing a "deadly dogged howl". The Duchess resists, however, and undermines Ferdinand's power by declaring that she is pleased by the torment: "nothing but noise and folly can keep me in my right wits".

Support for the idea that madness is presented as a fate worse than death can be found in the final scene of *A Streetcar Named Desire*. Blanche's mental instability provides the pretext for cruelty – such as the matron's suggestion that she be made to wear a straitjacket. Blanche is stripped of all autonomy, akin to an animal, as indicated by the matron's demeaning suggestion that "these fingernails have to be trimmed."

By contrast, the Duchess is able to retain some agency over her life, because she has possession of her mind. This is indicated by the fact that it is she, and not the distressed Bosola, who orders the executioners to "pull and pull strongly". In addition, she is able to proclaim her identity emphatically: "I am Duchess of Malfi still." Madness, however, forbids this self-possession; it destroys the **façade** of the refined and respectable southern belle which Blanche had endeavoured so desperately to create. Instead, she is described as "downright loco" and "nuts" by Stanley.

"Pull, and pull strongly, for your able strength must pull down heaven upon me…"

The Duchess of Malfi, Act IV scene ii

Indeed, it could even be suggested that the post-war society in which *A Streetcar Named Desire* is set actively attempts to force the identity of a 'madwoman' on Blanche, as a form of punishment for her promiscuity. This interpretation would be in keeping with what Williams himself told his agent, Audrey Wood, was the "one major theme" of his work: "the destructive power of society on the sensitive, non-conformist individual".

Perhaps Ferdinand is seeking to do the same thing when he attempts to destabilise his sister's mind, but the Duchess' strength and courage prevents him from succeeding here. Indeed, even her executioners are in awe of her strength; Bosola describes her as possessing a "behaviour so noble as gives a majesty to adversity". Whilst the Duchess is able to die with a degree of power and her name, therefore, madness – or, rather, being labelled as 'mad' – strips these from Blanche, leaving her wholly powerless.

Another Question:

In both plays, characters strive desperately for power over other characters. Is madness used as a tool to achieve this?

We touched on this idea just now, when we considered how Ferdinand attempts to destabilise the mind of his sister, and society attempts to punish Blanche for her promiscuity. But does it go even further than this?

The **antagonists** in both plays attempt to use madness as a tool to disempower the **protagonists**. There are some interesting links that can be made here. In both plays, for example, psychological attacks are launched through the giving of 'gifts': Ferdinand orders the executioners to deliver a coffin to the Duchess, in the hope of causing her distress, whilst Stanley hands Blanche a "ticket back to Laurel" on her birthday, which he knows will make her deeply anxious, having recently discovered her history of promiscuity and disgrace.

"Here is a present from your princely brothers, and may it arrive welcome, for it brings last benefit, last sorrow."

The Duchess of Malfi, Act VI scene ii

Williams uses Stanley's dialogue here to make his insensitivity appear particularly sinister: short, exclamatory sentences ("Ticket! Back to Laurel! On the Greyhound! Tuesday!") convey a sense of excitement and delight at the prospect of causing Blanche distress (indeed, this act of cruelty leaves her "coughing" and "gagging" in the bathroom).

Moreover, both antagonists use sound in an attempt to penetrate and unsettle the minds of their victims. The actor playing Stanley, for example, is likely to use the power of his voice to intimidate Blanche, and Williams indicates that he has a propensity for shouting by including capital letters in his **dialogue**: "Get *OUT* of the *BATHROOM*!"

Similarly, sound is also used as a form of psychological aggression in *The Duchess of Malfi*, albeit not by the brothers themselves. Instead, as we mentioned above, they arrange an "antimasque", during which the "madfolk" create an ominous and frightening atmosphere by singing a "deadly dogged howl". Though the Duchess remains sane, the antimasque could be interpreted as an outward manifestation of her inner turmoil – just as the "inhuman voices" and "lurid reflections" prior to the implied rape scene in *Streetcar* signify Blanche's inner terror. Through sound, speech and action, therefore, the antagonists in both plays actively seek to destabilise the minds of their victims.

Is madness presented as a complex and tragic phenomenon in *A Streetcar Named Desire*, but is merely a gruesome spectacle in *The Duchess of Malfi*?

T. S Eliot famously wrote that "Webster was much possessed by death", and his work is often considered to be gratuitously violent and bloody. It is easy to find evidence to support this view in *The Duchess of Malfi*; the audience witness a procession of gruesome horrors, from the artificial corpses and the dead man's hand, to the "antimasque" and Cariola's murder. This interpretation would also seem to suggest that madness, like violence, is depicted as a gruesome, horrific spectacle, intended to arouse excitement and horror from the audience.

Remind yourself of the key contextual information on page 39. *The Duchess of Malfi* belongs to the Renaissance genre of the revenge tragedy, inspired by the works of Seneca; plays of this kind are characterised by extreme violence, hyperbole and melodrama. Madness, therefore, is not intended to be tragically realistic, as it is in *A Steetcar Named Desire*, but a hyperbolic spectacle. Williams' more subtle depiction of mental illness, meanwhile, suggests an appreciation of it as a serious condition, which perhaps derives from personal experience: his sister, Rose, underwent a lobotomy, and was institutionalised for much of her life, whilst Williams himself suffered a nervous breakdown at the age of twenty-four.

Thus, this experience perhaps gave Williams an insight into the complex nature of mental illness. Blanche is not "loco" in the sense that the other characters believe she is. Stanley, along with Stella,

Mitch and Eunice, consider Blanche to be mad because she is detached from reality and believes in nonsensical fictions – such as the idea that the near-mythical Shep Huntleigh is coming to save her from destitution. What they fail to understand, therefore, is that Blanche does not – initially - believe these fictions; she knowingly invents them in order to make the world appear less terrifying and miserable (she wants "magic", not "realism"). Her 'madness', therefore, lies in the fact that, slowly, as the misery of her life becomes greater and more difficult to ignore, Blanche comes to believe her own fictions, forgetting that they are her own inventions. She loses her sense of what is real. The tragedy of *A Streetcar*

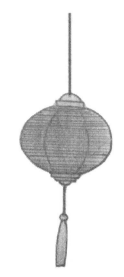

I've been onto you from the start! Not once did you pull any wool over this boy's eyes! You come in here and sprinkle the place with powder and spray perfume and cover the light-bulb with a paper lantern, and lo and behold the place has turned into Egypt and you are the Queen of the Nile!"

A Streetcar Named Desire,
Scene X

Named Desire (and what makes it, to borrow Arthur Miller's phrase, "a cry of pain") is that the one tool

Blanche has to alleviate her suffering – the ability to manipulate the truth – ends up destroying her mind.

> "Stanley, in his ignorance and insensitivity, destroys both Blanche's hope and her illusion. He sees through her pose without understanding why she needs one. He thinks merely that she feels superior to him and he wishes to destroy her composure to make her recognise that she is the same as he, a sexual animal."
>
> J. M. McGlinn
>
> From *Tennessee Williams: A Tribute*

By contrast, Webster's depiction of madness is almost comical. Ferdinand attempts to attack his own shadow, his "lycanthropia" causes him to howl like a wolf, whilst, in the final chaotic scene, he believes himself to be a horse: "Give me some whet hay, I am broken winded." This suggests that there are few parallels between the ways in which the two playwrights depict madness.

An alternative reading, however, might suggest that the above argument is a simplification of Webster's work. Michael Billington, for example, argues that there is more to *The Duchess of Malfi* than "a procession of morbid horrors". Though Ferdinand is a villainous antagonist and his madness is hyperbolic, there is perhaps something pitiable in it, which aligns it more with the madness of Blanche. His attempt to "throttle" his own shadow, for example – though often played in a comic, melodramatic fashion – could be considered a symbolic indication of his self-loathing, after having killed his "dearest friend". Indeed, this self-hatred is not unlike Blanche's perpetual bathing in an attempt to 'cleanse' herself of her past mistakes. Today, self-loathing is very closely linked to depression, a serious mental illness; perhaps Ferdinand's madness is not as anti-real and sensational as it first appears.

Similarly, just as there are traces of the realistic underlying the madness in *The Duchess of Malfi*, there are elements of sensationalism in Blanche's seemingly realistic mental instability. As is typical of the playwrights and artists of the early twentieth century, Williams' use of set, lighting, props and music are not intended to provide a realistic image of a two-storey flat in New Orleans. Rather, they serve a symbolic function, representing abstract concepts. Indeed, Williams referred to himself as a "symbolist".

This is demonstrated by his use of the Varsouviana (the polka tune to which Allan and Blanche were dancing immediately prior to his suicide) to indicate Blanche's psychological distress whenever she becomes troubled by the memory of her former husband. This music is not heard by the other characters; it is an impressionistic device used to show how Blanche is haunted, and psychologically troubled, by her past. Thus, both Webster and Williams combine realism and sensationalism in their presentations of madness.

"We danced the Varsouviana! Suddenly in the middle of the dance the boy I had married broke away from me and ran out of the casino. A few moments later – a shot!"

A Streetcar Named Desire, Scene VI

Family Relationships

The Duchess of Malfi and *A Streetcar Named Desire* present us with family relationships which are weak and unreliable. Indeed, it could even be suggested that the inability of the characters to confide in and support their relatives is responsible for the play's tragic conclusions.

Consider the following questions....

"You have bloodily approved the ancient truth

That kindred commonly do worse agree

Than remote strangers."

The Duchess of Malfi, Act IV scene ii

How far would you agree that strangers are more reliable than family members in *The Duchess Malfi* and *A Streetcar Named Desire*?

"Trust is entirely absent. The characters are well aware that, if they are to be safe, they can only rely upon themselves." In light of this comment, explore how Webster and Williams present family relationships in *The Duchess of Malfi* and *A Streetcar Named Desire*.

How far would you agree that Webster and Williams present us with an image of domestic life which is strikingly bleak, hostile and dangerous?

To what extent do you agree with the view that, "problems arise because family members do not truly understand one another" in *The Duchess of Malfi* and *A Streetcar Named Desire*?

"Relationships between siblings are characterised by a struggle for authority over one another." How far can this comment be applied to *The Duchess of Malfi* and *A Streetcar Named Desire*?

Something to consider:

Is familial love weaker than sexual passion in *The Duchess of Malfi* and *A Streetcar Named Desire*?

As we have already discussed, family relationships are weak in these plays, but it is interesting to consider why. One key reason, perhaps, is that the characters do not value familial love as greatly as they do sexual passion.

In *A Streetcar Named Desire*, for example, it is Stella's attraction to Stanley that leads her to betraying Blanche. This betrayal is perhaps foreshadowed in Scene IV, in which Stella claims that

> "...there are things that happen between a man and a woman in the dark – that sort of make everything else seem – unimportant."

Scene IV

This indicates that everything in Stella's life, including her sister, is inferior to her sexual passion. Look at how the dialogue here is fractured by hyphens, which slows the pace of her speech, creating a sense of wistful thoughtfulness, as if – at this moment – she is completely absorbed in the memory of her past sexual experiences with Stanley (indeed, Williams instructs the actress playing Stella to "pause" after delivering this line) This, again, indicates the overpowering nature of her desire.

Similarly, sexual desire could also be seen to destroy family relationships in *The Duchess of Malfi*, albeit, in this case, the desire is Ferdinand's implied incestuous feelings for his sister herself. Though it is important to remember that these feelings are only ever implied – incest is never directly alluded to in the play – it is a common interpretation of the text. The Globe Theatre's 2014 production of the play, directed by Dominic Dromgoole and starring David Dawson as Ferdinand, follows this interpretation, for example. It can also be inferred from Ferdinand's "wild...tempest" in Act II scene v, in which he imagines his sister in the "shameful act of sin" with a "strong-thighed bargeman". Indeed, Ferdinand's "intemperate anger" here even serves to shock the Cardinal: "Are you stark mad?"

Ferdinand's unhealthy obsession with his sister's body is indicated, furthermore, when he declares that he will "root up her goodly forests" and "lay her general territory as waste", since these are both sexual innuendos as well as violent threats; gardens and forests were common metaphors for the female body in poetry and drama during the Renaissance. The choice of the verb "lay", moreover, has particular sexual connotations. As it is this desire that leads Ferdinand to brutally torturing and murdering his sister, it is clear that his sexual jealousy is stronger than any familial love he may have for his "dearest friend". If this interpretation is accepted, therefore, it is certainly fair to conclude that sexual desire destroys family relationships in both plays, which in turn implies that the former is stronger than the latter. This, as we see, opens the door to tragedy.

The Family Home:

In neither play is the family home presented as a safe and comfortable environment; rather, it is always at risk of being invaded by the outside world. This is particularly important in *A Streetcar Named Desire*, because, as this is a play about domestic abuse, the home must not appear to be a domestic sanctuary.

One way in which Williams evokes this is through the set, which he describes, in his detailed opening stage directions, as consisting of a "two-storey corner building" and the surrounding street. By allowing the audience to see the outside street at all times during the play (as well as the voices that can be heard from it, such as the vendors shouting "Red hots!"), rather than confining their vision to the apartment, perhaps reinforces the idea that the home is not impermeable and self-contained. The interior world, Williams seems to suggest, is as harsh and dangerous as the urban exterior environment of post-war New Orleans.

Privacy and exclusivity are similarly absent in *The Duchess of Malfi*. The Duchess' home, akin to all the homes of the nobility in the seventeenth century, contains servants who overhear and eavesdrop. As Webster illustrates through Bosola, an unfaithful servant could lead to ruin. This idea is reinforced by Frances E. Dolman, who points out that the Renaissance household was "riddled with...co-habitants and neighbours [who] peeped and listened".

Indeed, even in the most harmonious domestic scene in the play, Act III scene ii - in which the Duchess and Antonio engage in sexual **repartee** before the intrusion of Ferdinand – Cariola is present, perhaps highlighting the impossibility of true privacy. The presentation of the home as a fragile space, vulnerable to intrusion, in both plays could be seen to underscore the broader theme of the instability of family life.

Approaching a Question

In the exam, you will choose one question from a selection of two – so don't panic. You have a little freedom if one of the questions does not appeal to you.

If you are in the lucky position of loving both questions, don't agonise over which one to choose – you simply do not have the time. Pick one and get started.

Read the question carefully:

Remember that there are both AO1 and AO5 marks available for addressing the question fully and consistently. It is crucial, therefore, that you do not overlook key words. Take the following example:

> "All of the characters are constantly struggling to secure power over one another." In light of this statement, examine how Webster and Williams depict sexual relationships in *The Duchess of Malfi* and *A Streetcar Named Desire*.

WJEC Eduqas usually include a statement or quotation in their questions (though not always). Under exam conditions, it would be easy to read the quotation above and move swiftly on to discuss the ways in which Ferdinand and the Cardinal control and exploit Bosola, or how Stanley wields power over Mitch. This, however, would be irrelevant, because the question is asking candidates to discuss how the playwrights present <u>sexual relationships</u>. It is essential, therefore, that you **always read and reread <u>every part</u> of the question** before you begin writing. Do not only read the quotation.

Silly mistakes happen in exams. To minimise the chances of you making them, ring round or underline the key words in a question, and make sure that you haven't missed anything.

Address the question fully:

The above section warns candidates against accidentally overlooking certain details in a question, but sometimes students do so deliberately. Consider the following example:

> "All of the characters are selfish, stubborn and cruel. It is difficult to sympathise with any of them, despite the obstacles they face." To what extent is this true of *The Duchess of Malfi* and *A Streetcar Named Desire*?

This is an example of a question with <u>multiple adjectives</u>: "selfish, stubborn and cruel." When this happens, an examiner is **not** inviting you to pick out and discuss the adjectives that appeal to you. Instead, <u>you are expected to address them all</u>, to some degree. **Never decide to answer half or part of a question**; doing this is a recipe for disaster.

Find the Grey Areas:

Exam questions can often be very one-sided, or black-and-white. One feature of A/A* level essays is that they tend to pick out and discuss the nuances, or 'grey areas', in a question.

Take a look at the next page for an example of a question that has been "picked part" in this way.

Always look out for nouns which group multiple characters together, such as "women", "men", or the word "characters" itself. Whilst the characters in both plays have certain things in common with each other, there are also many differences, and no two are identical. It is likely that they will not all conform to the description in the question. Try to pick out exceptions to the rule, if you can.

Remember to look beyond the obvious; whilst there is much that you can (and should) discuss about Blanche and the Duchess here, the statement is making a broad assertion about "females" in general. What about Stella, Julia or Eunice? Be aware that there is a fine line between looking beyond the obvious and diverging off topic – a discussion of whether male characters are innocent victims, for example, would not be relevant here.

"Females in *The Duchess of Malfi* and *A Streetcar Named Desire* are not innocent victims, but rather knowing women who invite their own fates."

This is an interesting adjective. If we agree with the idea that females tempt their own fates (and you may not), do we agree that they do so 'knowingly'? Instead, they could be considered naïve characters, who unwittingly cause themselves suffering.

Is it possible to be a victim without being wholly innocent? Could we not conclude that, whilst female characters do make mistakes which sometimes serve to "invite their own fate", they are still ultimately victims of cruelty and misfortune?

Breaking down a question in this way will help you to find different ideas to discuss in your essay, and will make your overall argument more insightful and sophisticated.

Try annotating the following questions:

"The characters in the plays are either wholly good or wholly evil. It is a strict dichotomy; there is no in-between." In light of this quotation, explore connections between *The Duchess of Malfi* and *A Streetcar Named Desire*.

How far would you agree with the view that, "ambition is the sole cause of tragedy and suffering" in *The Duchess of Malfi* and *A Streetcar Named Desire*?

"The social hierarchies in both plays are shown to be rigid and implacable. They are challenged but they remain intact." To what extent is this true of *The Duchess of Malfi* and *A Streetcar Named Desire*?

How far would you agree that, in *The Duchess of Malfi* and *A Streetcar Named Desire*, Webster and Williams "endorse misogynistic attitudes by presenting women as deceitful and unstable individuals, who actively seek to cause chaos"?

"There is no moral lesson to be learnt from these plays. Webster and Williams only intend to show us the cruelty of the world, in which there is no kindness, honesty, or hope." To what extent is this true of *The Duchess of Malfi* and *A Streetcar Named Desire*?

After you have broken down the question, which will hopefully provide you with a few ideas, you are ready to plan.

Essay Planning

Writing practice essays can be a time-consuming and laborious way to revise. Though it is essential that you write a few full essays (ideally, your teacher should be setting these regularly), writing essay plans is an excellent way to revise.

Please note that revision essay plans are not the same as 'real' essay plans, which you write in an exam. A revision essay plan is a condensed version of a full essay; here is an example below. **You will not have time to write an essay plan of this length in the real exam**.

How far do you agree with the view that *The Duchess of Malfi* and *A Streetcar Named Desire* "are moral plays, intended to warn their audiences against the dangers of telling lies."

Introduction: In both plays, secrets relating to sex are kept by women and exposed by men. In both cases, the result is suffering and tragedy. The Duchess is murdered, whilst Blanche is sent to an institution for the mentally ill. This seems to

---

suggest that these plays are indeed intended to "warn their audiences against the dangers of telling lies". Alternatively, it could be suggested that the playwrights actually support their protagonists, and argue that it is not always morally wrong to deceive.

Paragraph One: Both Blanche and the Duchess keep secrets, and suffer as a result:

- Both playwrights show their protagonists deceiving others in the very first scene (Blanche tells Stella that she "rarely touch[es]" alcohol, the Duchess tells her brothers that she will "never marry").
- They intentionally deceive others, regardless of the consequences. Brian Gibbons points out that "the Duchess anticipates moral condemnation" in this scene, because she tells the audience that she must keep her intentions a secret, or else "old wives" might report that she "winked and chose a husband".
- They both suffer: the Duchess is tortured and killed, whilst Blanche is committed to an institution. This seems to suggest that the playwrights are having their characters punished for their lies, which in turns supports the view that they are trying to teach their audiences a moral lesson.

Paragraph Two: Alternatively, it could be suggested that deceit is not always presented as being morally wrong in these plays:

- Michael Billington argues that Blanche lies to protect herself against "solitude and desperation". She wants "magic" instead of "realism" because the real world is too painful for her to inhabit.
- This sympathetic view of secrecy and deceit is perhaps the result of personal experience (homosexuality was a felony in the 1940s, and thus Williams, like Blanche, was forced to conceal his sexuality).
- Deceit allows the Duchess and Antonio to maintain their happy marriage ("I prithee when were we so merry?").
- The Duchess pretends that Antonio has wronged her in an attempt to save his life. This is described as "noble lie" – an oxymoronic phrase which suggests that deceit can be put to honourable purposes.

Paragraph Three: Indeed, it is those who attempt to expose secrets who are presented in a negative light, rather than those who keep them.

- The antagonists in both plays are made deeply insecure by the possibility of secrets escaping their attention.
- Williams shows this by using props as symbols – a device commonly used by the modern playwrights of the early twentieth century. Blanche's trunk represents her past (or her "life luggage", to borrow Jackie Shead's phrase). Stanley's search through it in Scene II marks the beginning of his quest to expose the secrets of her past. By Scene X, the trunk "hangs open", indicating that Blanche has been fully exposed and ruined.
- Ferdinand and the Cardinal employ Bosola to spy on the Duchess. The presence of Bosola in the Duchess' home means that it never appears a comfortable or safe domestic sanctuary. As Frances E. Dolman points out, the audience always have a sense that "co-habitants and neighbours" are "peep[ing] and listen[ing]".
- Thus, the antagonists are depicted as overbearing, manipulative characters, for whom the audience are encouraged to lack sympathy. This suggests that the playwrights are not inviting their audiences to show disdain for liars, but for those who expose liars.

Conclusion: It is difficult to sustain the argument that Webster and Williams are encouraging us to criticise, and learn from, the mistakes of Blanche and the Duchess. Ultimately, both playwrights seem to suggest that deceit is their only option – it does not characterise them as foolish or corrupt, but reinforces their vulnerability.

This is a really worthwhile revision task, because it encourages you to draw connections across the plays, and consider relevant AO3 and AO5 material to draw into discussions.

Flick through this guide and have a look at the questions which open each of the chapters on "Key Themes". Pick a few and write essay plans like the one above on blank sheets of paper. At first, use the plays and your notes to include important quotations, critical material and context. When you are feeling more confident, try to write some plans using quotations, critics and contextual information which you have learnt, without using the plays or your notes.

Clearly, you will not have time to write a detailed plan like this in the real exam. Instead, your plan will probably look something like this:

> How far do you agree with the view that *The Duchess of Malfi* and *A Streetcar Named Desire* "are moral plays, intended to warn their audiences against the dangers of telling lies."
>
> **Paragraph One:** Both Blanche and the Duchess keep secrets, and suffer as a result
>
> **Paragraph Two:** deceit is not always presented as being morally wrong
>
> **Paragraph Three:** Those who expose secrets appear more villainous than those who keep them.

Writing a plan like this in the exam will help to keep you focussed on the question, and ensure that your essay shows evidence of organisation. It will also help you to make your paragraphs comparative; as we discussed in the "Addressing AO4" section, you must never devote a whole paragraph to one play.

Writing short plans like this is another helpful revision task. Flick through this guide and find some more questions that you have not written an answer to yet, and simulate the first 5-10 minutes of an exam by picking apart the question and writing a plan like the one above.

Writing your Essay

There is no magic formula for writing a good essay, and you will know what works best for you. Nevertheless, here are some key points to steer you in the right direction:

- In general, writing fewer well-developed paragraphs is better than writing many short paragraphs. This is particularly the case in this paper, because you have two plays to write about and many different assessment objectives to address. Look at the sample essay on page 152 – this has only three paragraphs, as well as an introduction and a conclusion, but they are detailed and well-developed.

- However, when you are writing your long paragraphs, be careful not to digress from the question. You must remain focussed; as previously mentioned, there are AO1 and AO5 marks available for answering the question. You cannot afford to neglect it.

- This also means that you cannot regurgitate pre-learned material which is irrelevant or only vaguely relevant - examiners will spot this a mile off. Only refer to points that you have written in practice essays if they are <u>wholly</u> and <u>entirely</u> relevant in light of the question.

- Remember that AO4 is worth 20 marks; connections must guide the structure of your essay (see page 18).

- Whilst, again, there is no magic formula for a good essay, this structure might help you to start thinking about what to write and how to draw all of the different information together:

<u>First Sentence:</u> A point which spans across both plays.
For example: *The antagonists in both plays attempt to use madness as a tool to disempower the protagonists.*

<u>Then:</u> Closer analysis (AO2) and tight, focussed links (AO4).
For example: *One way in which Williams and Webster indicate this is through their use of sound. The actor playing Stanley, for example, is likely to use the power of his voice to intimidate Blanche. Indeed, Williams suggests that Stanley has a propensity for shouting by including capital letters in his dialogue: "Get OUT of the*

BATHROOM!" Similarly, sound is also used as a form of aggression in The Duchess of Malfi, albeit not by the brothers themselves. Instead, they arrange an "antimasque", in which the "madfolk" enter the stage and create an ominous and frightening atmosphere by singing a "deadly dogged howl".

Then: Draw in relevant AO3 or AO5 material
For example: The antimasque is a gruesome parody of the court masque, a form of entertainment in the Renaissance. The horror of the scene may well have resonated more with a contemporary audience, because they would have seen it as subverting a traditionally pleasant activity, with which they were familiar, into a horrific spectacle.

Final Sentence: Make a concluding point which spans across both plays
For example: Through sound and intimidation, therefore, the antagonists in both plays actively seek to destabilise the minds of their victims.

By following this structure, you can ensure that your paragraph prioritises drawing connections between the two plays, which is vital given that AO4 is worth 20 marks. Though AO5 is not included in the above example, this is not a major issue because this is only a single paragraph. AO5 <u>must</u> be addressed elsewhere in the essay.

Similarly, language analysis would ideally be more in-depth and detailed than this for the highest AO2 marks. Again, however, this is only a single, broken-down paragraph, so it is not a major issue.

See the next page for a sample essay, which draws together all of the assessment objectives.

Sample Essay

Below is the question that we picked apart on page 137 and an example of a high-level answer that has been written in response to it. A helpful exercise would be to highlight areas of the essay which clearly show AO2, AO3, AO4 and AO5 (AO1 is more difficult to pick out, as it is demonstrated by the overall tone of the piece, rather than by specific words or phrases). Alternatively, you could act like an examiner by writing "AO2", "AO3", "AO4" or "AO5" in the margin when you identify it.

"Females in *The Duchess of Malfi* and *A Streetcar Named Desire* are not innocent victims, but rather knowing women who invite their own fates." To what extent do you agree with this view?

The characters of *The Duchess of Malfi* and *A Streetcar Named Desire* are often morally ambiguous. Indeed, Tennessee Williams himself wrote, in an imaginary interview with himself entitled "The World I Live In", that "no man has a monopoly on right or virtue", nor "a corner on duplicity and evil". Rather, we are all a combination of the two. This philosophy runs through

Webster's work as well as that of Williams; both Blanche and the Duchess are victims of cruelty and misfortune, but in both cases it is made clear that they also serve to tempt their own tragic fates – by breaking cultural norms, for example. This ambiguity makes the matter of their culpability highly dependent on individual interpretation.

Both playwrights present female leads who bring disorder into their respective worlds by violating social and cultural norms. Blanche, for example, challenges convention through her promiscuity as an unmarried woman. Moreover, she attempts to find romance in young men, contravening the social codes of the 20th century, and indeed today, regarding relationships with children. Similarly, the Duchess also breaches social norms through her misplaced sexual desires, by marrying beneath her. This would have been considered – by a contemporary, Renaissance audience – to violate the Great Chain of Being; an originally classical concept which held that the universe has a hierarchical structure that has been fixed in place by God. There is a sacrilegious element to the Duchess' choice of an unnatural husband, therefore, which perhaps serves to support the argument that she acts to tempt her tragic fate. In addition, both characters break these codes "knowingly". This is illustrated by the fact that Blanche, after attempting to seduce the "young man" with literary allusions (she compares him to an "Arabian prince" from the *Arabian Nights*, for example), admits that she "must be good and keep my hands off children", thus indicating that she knows her behaviour to be disapproved of and wrong. In the same way, the Duchess acts knowingly, because she declares, in soliloquy, that she must keep her intentions a secret or else "old wives" will report that she "winked and chose a husband". As Brian Gibbons points out, this illuminating comment reveals that "the Duchess anticipates moral condemnation", but decides to act rashly nevertheless. Thus, both Blanche and the Duchess wilfully defy cultural norms, which perhaps serves to tempt their fates.

Alternatively, however, it could be suggested that, far from being the "knowing" authors of their own fates, Blanche and the Duchess are naïve characters who unwittingly cause their own suffering. Though the Duchess poses a serious challenge to the established order by contravening the Great Chain of Being, for example, she does not appear to know it: "I have not gone about this to create any new world or custom". Similarly, Blanche demonstrates her innocence through her reliance on men; she describes Mitch as a "cleft in the rock of the word that I could hide in", and, the morning after the "Poker Night" scene (during which Stanley beats his pregnant wife), Blanche looks to the "gentleman" Shep Huntleigh as a means of escape: "Darling Shep. Sister and I in desperate situation…" Williams emphasises the futility of this by characterising the men of the play – to borrow Simon Bubb's phrase – not as "active agents of redemption from […] suffering, but as its cause." By looking to men for help, rather than herself, Blanche accentuates her problems, rather than relieving them. Thus, whilst both characters "invite their own fates", it is, arguably, not knowingly done.

Even this more sympathetic reading, however, maintains that it is ultimately Blanche and the Duchess who are at fault for their suffering – and this view seems incongruous with the representation of society in both plays. Indeed, both playwrights appear critical of social and cultural norms, rather than the women who defy them. In particular, both Webster and Williams are critical of patriarchal prejudices, as signified by the attention they draw towards gender-based double standards. The Cardinal, for example, claims, whilst he is participating in an affair with Julia, that he would need "that fantastic glass invented by Galileo" to find "a constant woman", just as Mitch claims that Blanche is "not clean enough" to be his wife, before attempting to rape her. By drawing attention to these moments of hypocrisy, therefore, both playwrights seem to suggest that, whilst the females in both plays may not be wholly "innocent", as the above arguments reveal, they are still very much "victims" of patriarchal prejudices. Indeed, this reading seems particularly apt in the case of *The Duchess of Malfi* when we consider Webster's handling of his source material, which provides an insight into his sympathies for the Duchess. Webster was inspired by William Painter's "Duchess of Malfy", in which the Duchess, Giovanna d'Aragona, is described as a "foolish woman" who married in order to "glut her libidinous appetite". This, therefore, is clearly very different from Webster's Duchess, who is depicted as honourable in her defiance of her villainous brothers: "a behaviour so noble as gives a majesty to adversity". Thus, by refusing to conform to the misogynistic foundations laid out by Painter, Webster appears to sympathise with the Duchess, which in turn suggests that she is an "innocent victim" rather than a "knowing" perpetrator.

To conclude, it is clear that both the Duchess and Blanche are responsible for committing rash acts which often serve to "invite their own fate[s]". However, it seems wrong to imply – as the statement possibly does – that, simply because these actions result in suffering, they are inherently foolish. Conversely, both Webster and Williams seems to suggest that Blanche and the Duchess are right and, indeed, courageous in their respective struggles against oppression and injustice, regardless of whether this struggle is – ultimately – doomed to fail.

Good Points:

This essay is of a very high standard because it is consistently comparative and makes some very interesting points. It has picked apart the question and examined some of the "grey areas" – such as whether "females" are necessarily the "knowing" authors of their own fates. It is fluently written, with an academic style and register. There is evidence of both context and alternative interpretations.

To Improve…

It would have been nice if the candidate had expanded the focus beyond Blanche and the Duchess and considered whether other "females", such as Stella, Julia and Eunice, act to invite the tragedies in both plays. Nevertheless, examiners understand that students are under time pressure, and the candidate has explored his/her points fully. It is better to have a few well-developed points than many under-developed ones, so perhaps the candidate has used the time allowed wisely in not addressing this.

To push their AO2 mark that bit higher, the candidate could have analysed some specific words or phrases from the plays (this is known as 'microanalysis', or close analysis). Nevertheless, this essay contains some excellent 'macro-analysis' (analysis of the plays as a whole).

Glossary

Allusion – a reference (*"He made an allusion to Shakespeare"*).

Anachronistic – attributing something to a period to which it does not belong. For example, it would be anachronistic to refer to John Webster as a feminist, because the feminist movement did not exist when Webster was alive.

Antagonist – The character who opposes, or is hostile towards, the main character (known as the protagonist).

Bourgeois – Typical or characteristic of the upper and middle classes.

Canon – In the literary world, the "canon" refers to a collection of works considered to be the most important or influential (*"Hamlet is a canonical play"*).

Climax – The high-point in the action of a story; the most exciting or important moment.

Denouement – The end of a story, in which everything is explained and concluded (Denouement is French for "unknotting").

Dialogue – a conversation between characters in a book, play or film

Didactic – offering instruction or teaching (*"the didactic play instructs its audience to be wary of flatterers"*).

Ellipsis – a series of dots (...), which are usually used in quotations to indicate that a section of the original text has been omitted.

Eponymous – the person or character after whom the work is named. For example, Jane Eyre is the eponymous heroine of the novel *Jane Eyre*. The Duchess of Malfi, moreover, is the eponymous protagonist in *The Duchess of Malfi*.

Façade – a deceptive, or false, outward appearance (*"She concealed her resentment with a friendly façade"*).

Foil – a person, character or thing which contrasts with (and so emphasises the qualities of) another

Foreshadow – to hint or indicate a future event (*"the storm foreshadowed the impending disaster"*).

Imperative Verb – verbs which issue a command (such as *"Sit"*, *"Listen"*, or *"Run!"*).

Lexical Field – a collection of related words; for example, a lexical field of disease might be *"pestilent"*, *"sickly"*, *"rotten"*, and *"decay"*.

Madonna-Whore Complex – The depiction of women in literature as either compassionate, pure, obedient virgins ("Madonnas") or sinful, wanton and untrustworthy prostitutes ("Whores"), with no in-between.

Malcontent – a character, in early modern drama, who is unhappy with the social structure and disapproves of other characters. The malcontent often comments on the play from the position of an outsider. Bosola performs this role in *The Duchess of Malfi*.

Metaphor – a figure of speech which compares a person or object with something that it does not literally resemble, in order to suggest similarities (*"The city was a jungle"*, *"life is a roller coaster"*).

Motif – a symbol which recurs or is repeated in a text.

Nuance – a subtle difference or distinction

Oxymoron – a combination of contradictory words, such as *"bitter sweet"*, or *"deafening silence"*.

Personification – a personified object is something that is not human, but which is given human qualities or characteristics; for example, *"the trees shivered fearfully in the wind"*. It can also refer to a human character who is intended to represent an abstract quality (*"he is the personification of greed"*).

Proletariat – the lower or working class

Protagonist – the leading, or main, character in a play or novel.

Repartee – a conversation consisting of quick, witty comments.

Simile – A figure of speech which compares one thing with something else, through the use of comparative words, such as "like" or "as" (*"as innocent as a child"*).

Social Darwinism – The theory that people in society are subject to the laws of natural selection ("survival of the fittest") that Charles Darwin had observed in the natural world. This theory, therefore, holds that 'weak' human beings, races and cultures will die out, or be crushed by, 'stronger' human beings, races and cultures. Though largely discredited today, this theory fascinated intellectuals in the late nineteenth and early twentieth century; it was also used to justify colonialism, imperialism and racism.

Soliloquy – a speech which reveals a character's internal thoughts, and is unheard by any other characters present on the stage.

Symbol – Something, such as an image or a word, which is used to represent something else.

Was this guide useful?

Notable is a brand new company, so we really appreciate all the feedback and advice we can get!

Tell us what you think by emailing us at admin@notableguides.co.uk, or contact us through social media:

@notableguides

@notable_guides

Our followers have access to news, offers, and study tips, as well as the opportunity to vote on what we write next!

Notable
www.notableguides.co.uk

Printed in Great Britain
by Amazon